D1287678

GRAPHIC SCIENCE

THE SOLID TRUTH ABOUT
STATES OF MATTER

WITH **MAX AXIOM**
SUPER SCIENTIST

by Agnieszka Biskup

illustrated by Cynthia Martin and Barbara Schulz

Consultant:
Christopher J. Conklin
Chemist, Aldrich Chemical
Member, American Chemical Society
Washington, D.C.

Capstone
press

Mankato, Minnesota

Graphic Library is published by Capstone Press,
151 Good Counsel Drive, P.O. Box 669, Mankato, Minnesota 56002.
www.capstonepub.com

Printed in the United States of America in Stevens Point, Wisconsin.
0072010
005865R

Books published by Capstone Press are manufactured with paper
containing at least 10 percent post-consumer waste.

Library of Congress Cataloging-in-Publication Data
Biskup, Agnieszka.
    The solid truth about states of matter with Max Axiom super scientist / by Agnieszka
Biskup; illustrated by Cynthia Martin and Barbara Schulz.
        p. cm. — (Graphic Library. Graphic Science)
    Includes bibliographical references and index.
    Summary: "In graphic novel format, follows the adventures of Max Axiom as he
explains the science behind states of matter" — Provided by publisher.
        ISBN-13: 978-1-4296-2339-1 (hardcover)
        ISBN-10: 1-4296-2339-X (hardcover)
        ISBN-13: 978-1-4296-3451-9 (softcover)
        ISBN-10: 1-4296-3451-0 (softcover)
        1. Matter — Juvenile literature. I. Martin, Cynthia, 1961- ill. II. Schulz, Barbara
(Barbara Jo), ill. III. Title. IV. Series.
    QC173.36.B49 2009
    530.4 — dc22   2008028694

Set Designer
Bob Lentz

Book Designer
Alison Thiele

Cover Artists
Tod Smith and Krista Ward

Colorist
Michael Kelleher

Editor
Lori Shores

Photo illustration credits:
BigStockPhoto.com/Joeshmo, 11; Shutterstock/Julien Grondin, 15; Shutterstock/Paul Paladin, 7

TABLE OF CONTENTS

SECTION 1

MATTER, ATOMS, AND MOLECULES ---- 4

SECTION 2

SOLIDS, LIQUIDS, AND GASES --------- 12

SECTION 3

MELTING, BOILING, AND FREEZING ---- 16

SECTION 4

EVAPORATION AND CONDENSATION - 22

More about States of Matter and Max Axiom 28–29
Glossary 30
Read More 31
Internet Sites 31
Index 32

SECTION 1 MATTER, ATOMS, AND MOLECULES

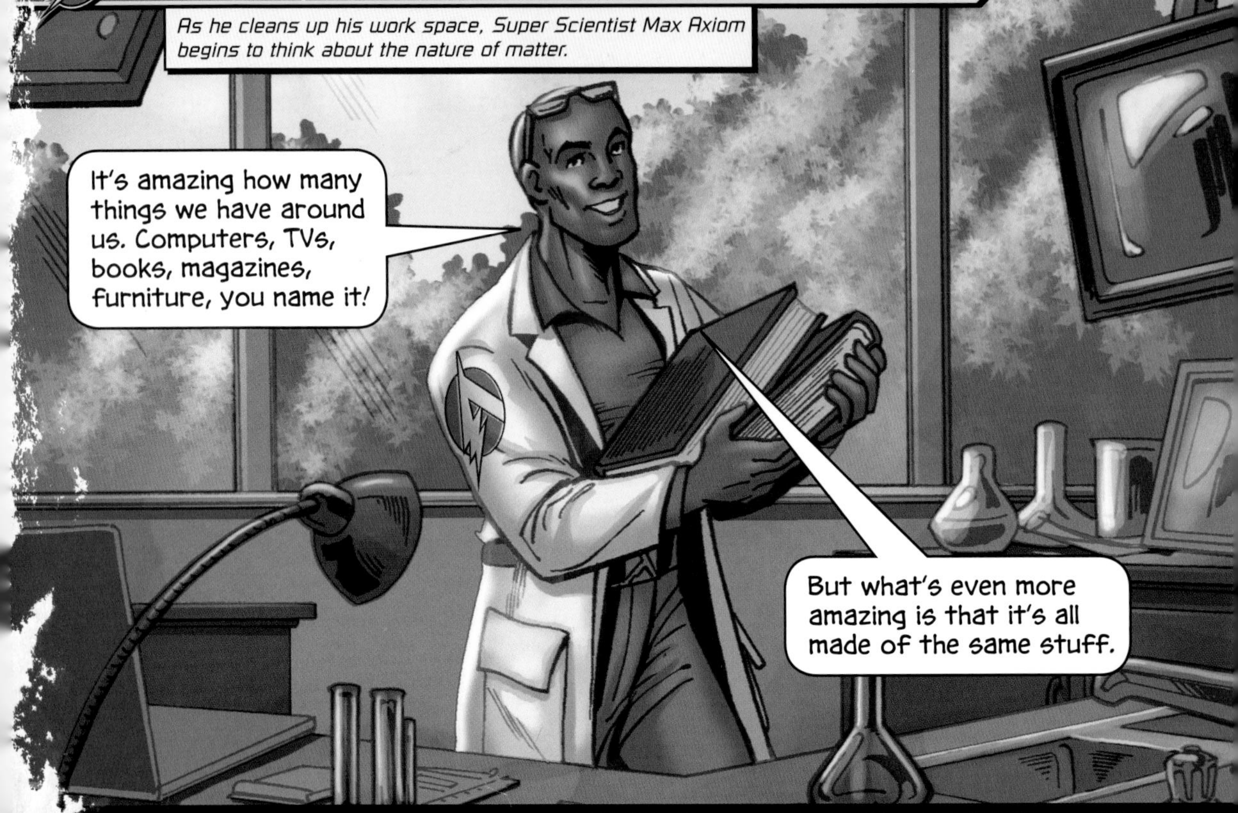
As he cleans up his work space, Super Scientist Max Axiom begins to think about the nature of matter.
It's amazing how many things we have around us. Computers, TVs, books, magazines, furniture, you name it!
But what's even more amazing is that it's all made of the same stuff.

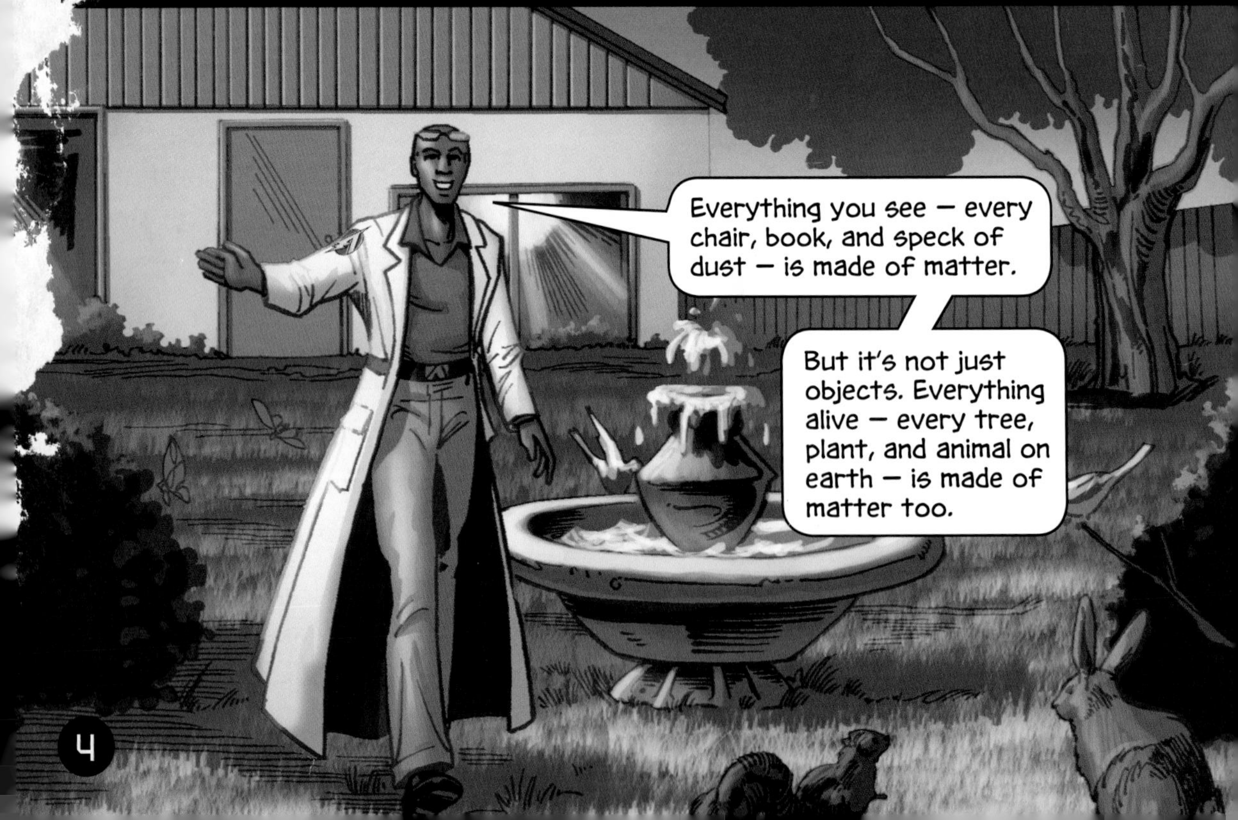
Everything you see — every chair, book, and speck of dust — is made of matter.
But it's not just objects. Everything alive — every tree, plant, and animal on earth — is made of matter too.

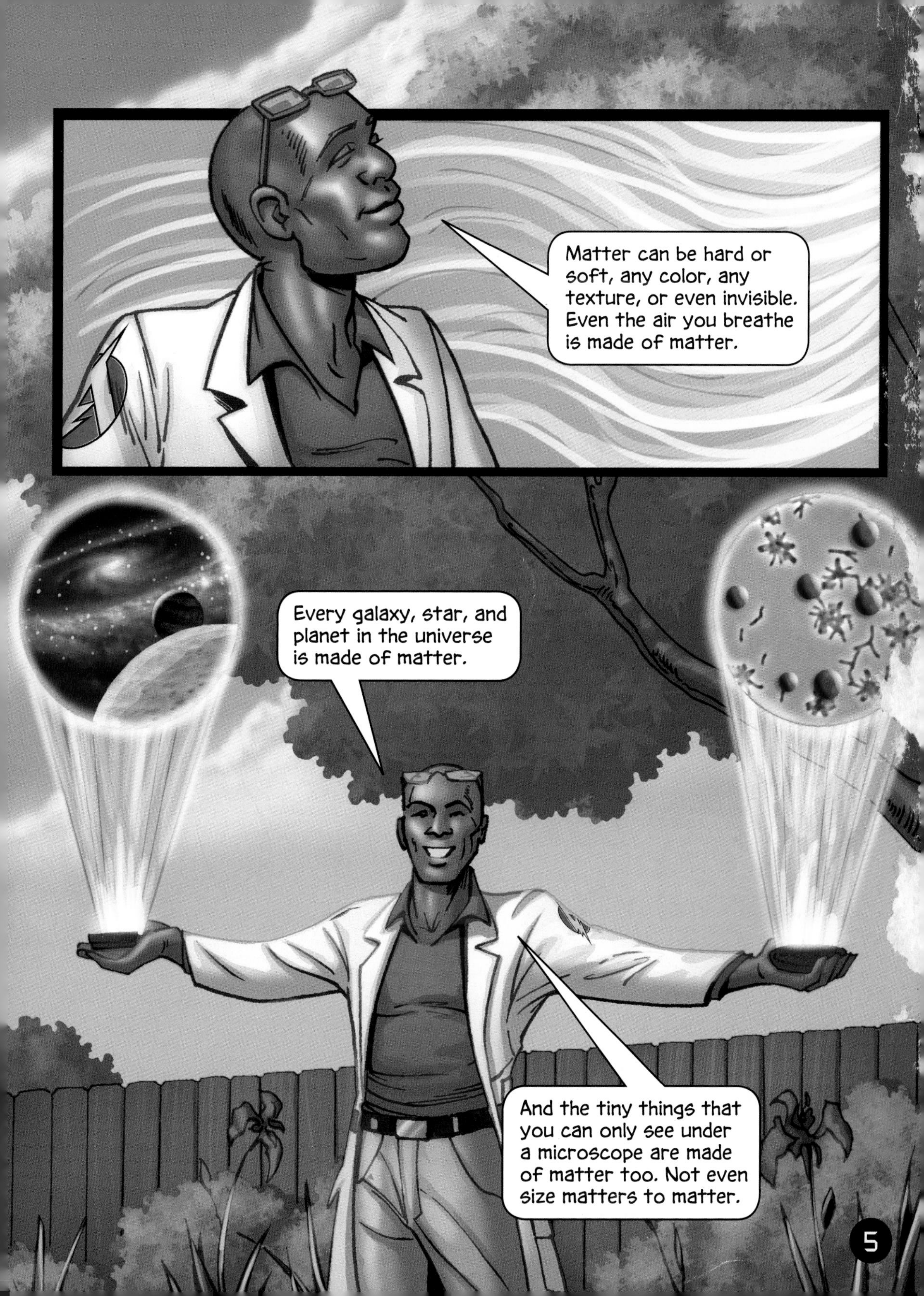
Matter can be hard or soft, any color, any texture, or even invisible. Even the air you breathe is made of matter.
Every galaxy, star, and planet in the universe is made of matter.
And the tiny things that you can only see under a microscope are made of matter too. Not even size matters to matter.

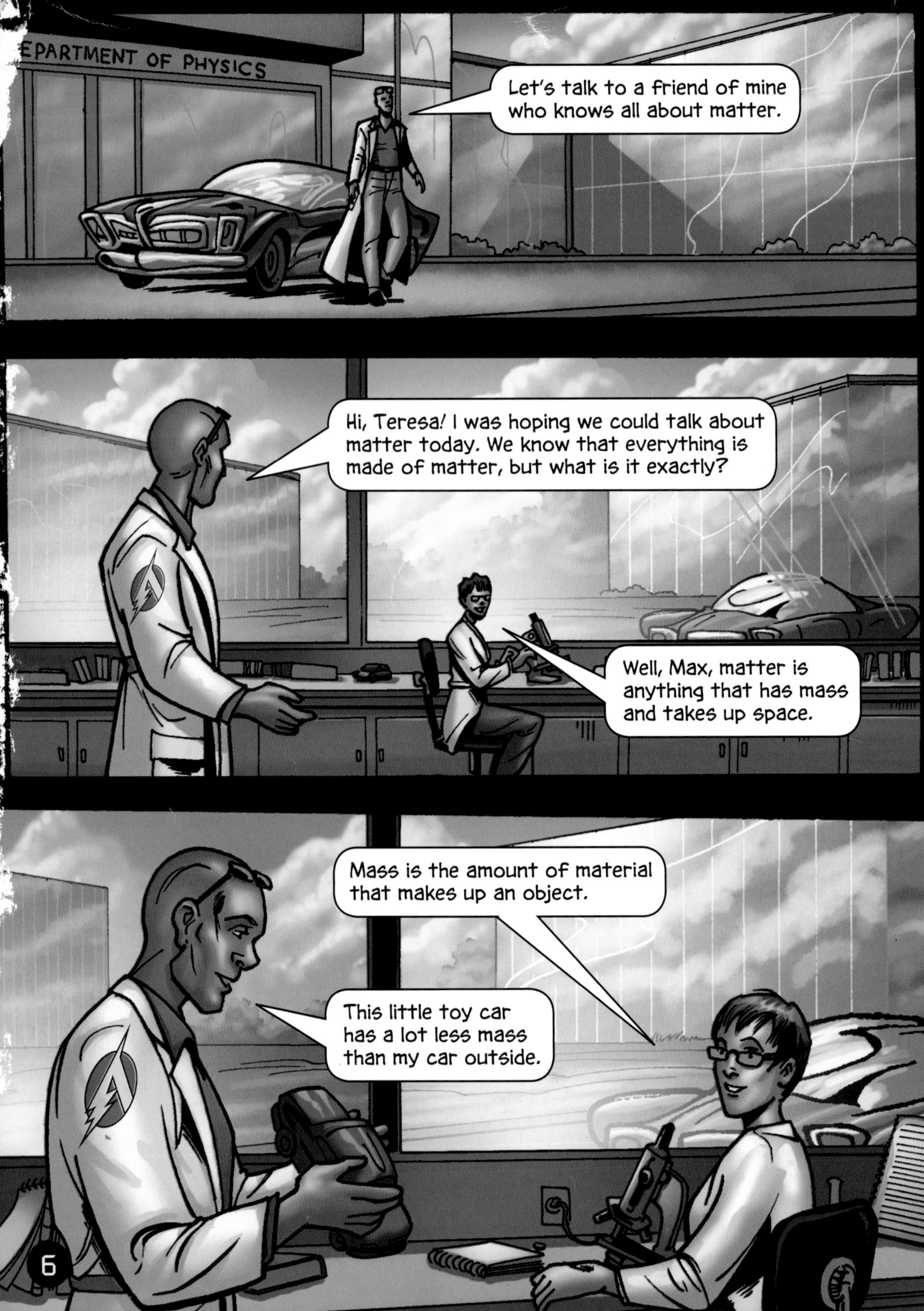
EPARTMENT OF PHYSICS
Let's talk to a friend of mine who knows all about matter.
Hi, Teresa! I was hoping we could talk about matter today. We know that everything is made of matter, but what is it exactly?
Well, Max, matter is anything that has mass and takes up space.
Mass is the amount of material that makes up an object.
This little toy car has a lot less mass than my car outside.

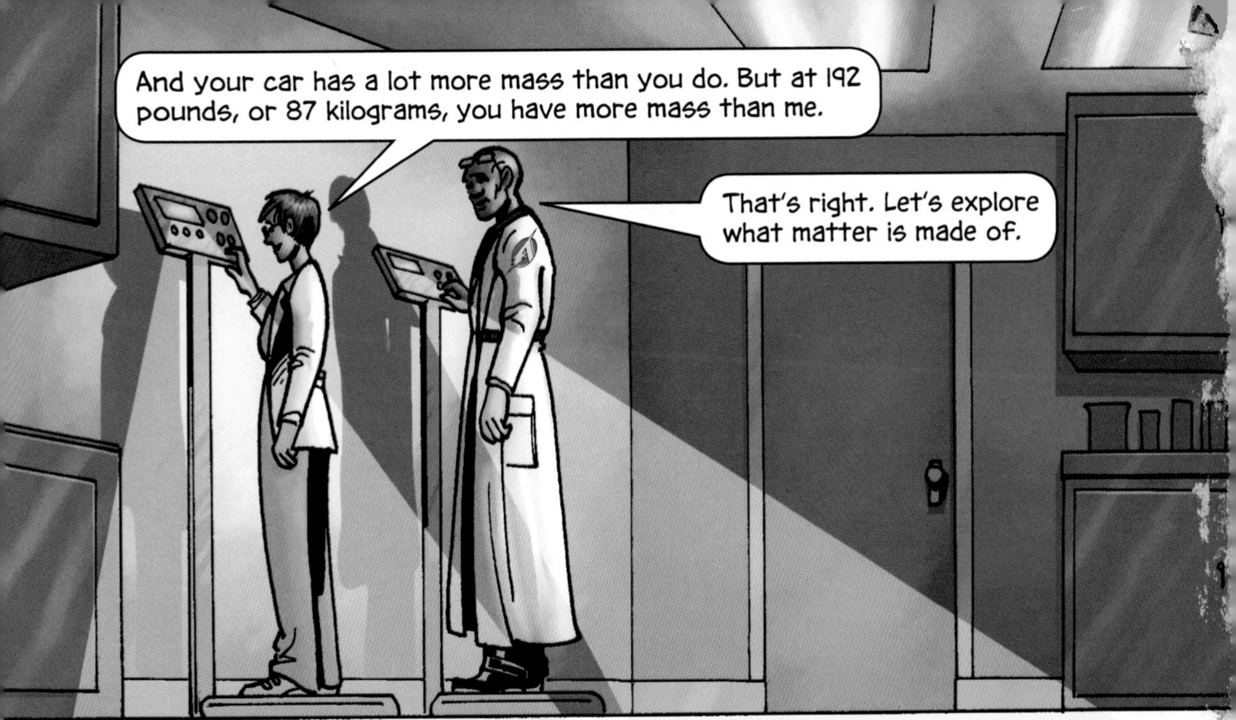
And your car has a lot more mass than you do. But at 192 pounds, or 87 kilograms, you have more mass than me.
That's right. Let's explore what matter is made of.

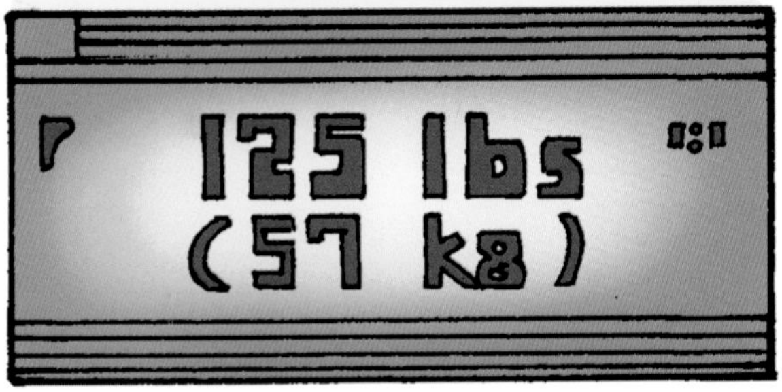
125 lbs
(57 kg)

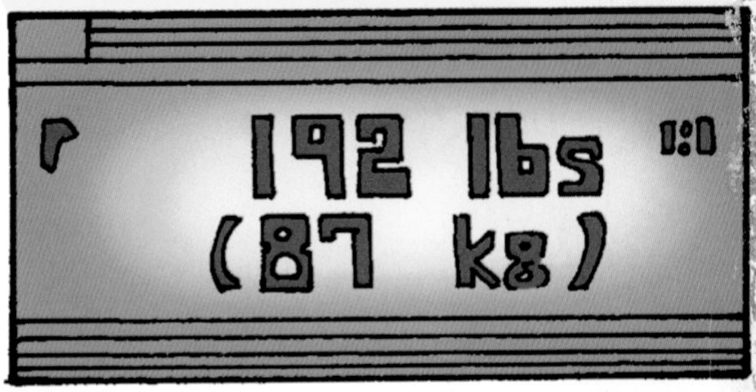
192 lbs
(87 kg)

MASS AND WEIGHT

ACCESS GRANTED: MAX AXIOM

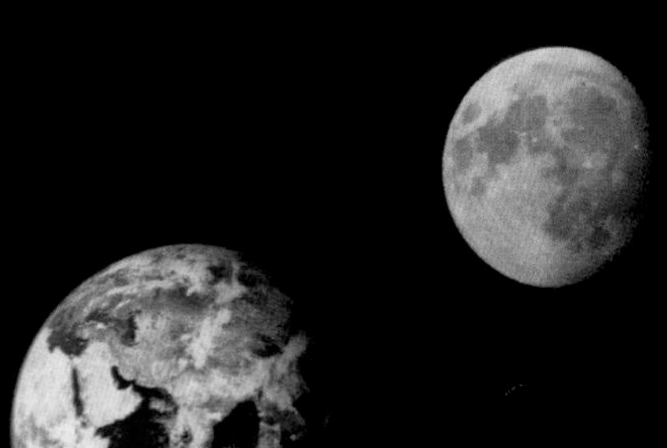

We usually think of mass and weight as being the same thing, but they really aren't. Weight is the measure of the pull of earth's gravity on an object. On the moon, an object would weigh only one-sixth of what it would weigh on earth. For example, a 12-pound (5.4 -kilogram) bowling ball would only weigh 2 pounds (1 kilogram) on the moon. Although the weights would be different, the mass would be the same.

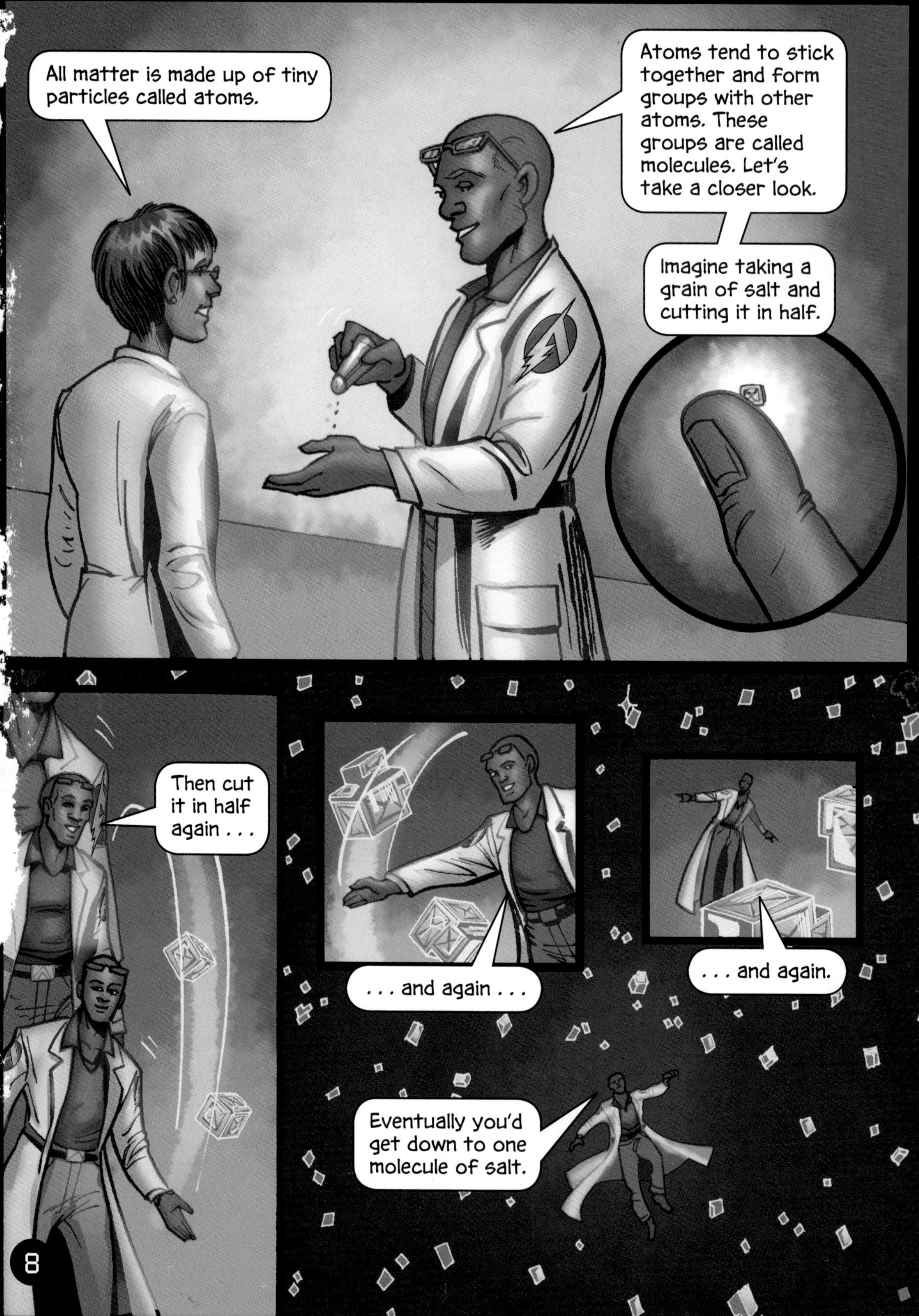
All matter is made up of tiny particles called atoms.
Atoms tend to stick together and form groups with other atoms. These groups are called molecules. Let's take a closer look.
Imagine taking a grain of salt and cutting it in half.
Then cut it in half again . . .
. . . and again . . .
. . . and again.
Eventually you'd get down to one molecule of salt.

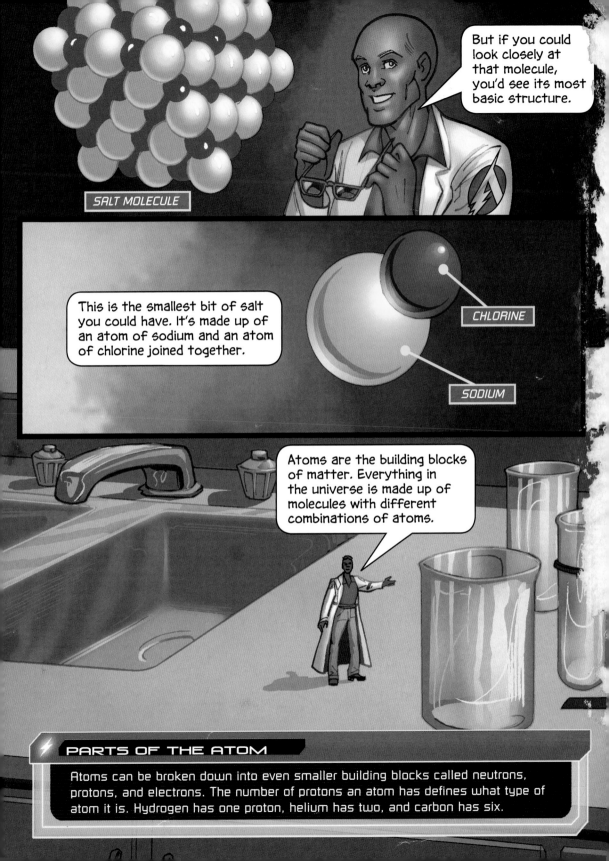

SALT MOLECULE

But if you could look closely at that molecule, you'd see its most basic structure.

CHLORINE

SODIUM

This is the smallest bit of salt you could have. It's made up of an atom of sodium and an atom of chlorine joined together.

Atoms are the building blocks of matter. Everything in the universe is made up of molecules with different combinations of atoms.

PARTS OF THE ATOM

Atoms can be broken down into even smaller building blocks called neutrons, protons, and electrons. The number of protons an atom has defines what type of atom it is. Hydrogen has one proton, helium has two, and carbon has six.

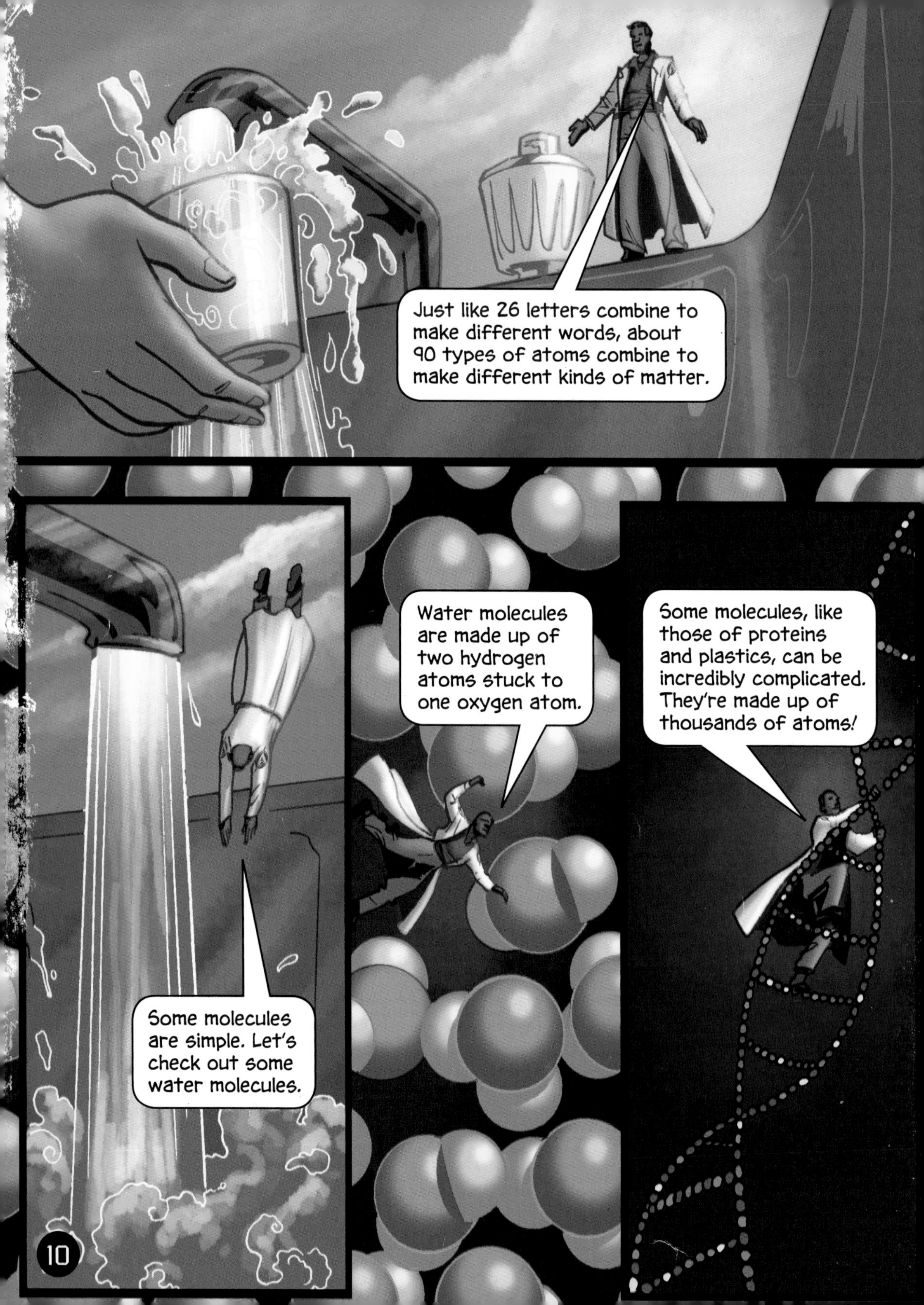
Just like 26 letters combine to make different words, about 90 types of atoms combine to make different kinds of matter.
Some molecules are simple. Let's check out some water molecules.
Water molecules are made up of two hydrogen atoms stuck to one oxygen atom.
Some molecules, like those of proteins and plastics, can be incredibly complicated. They're made up of thousands of atoms!

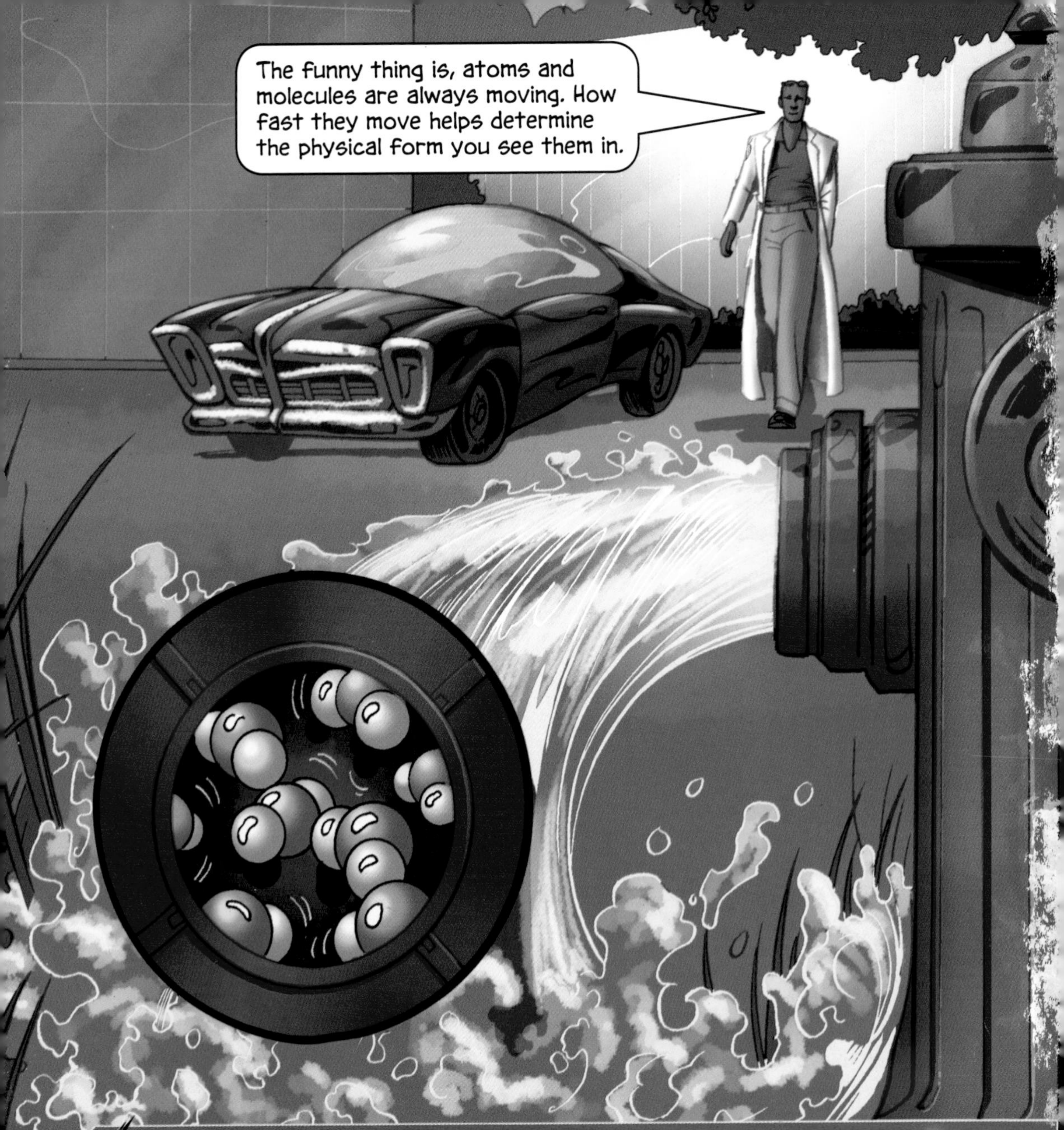

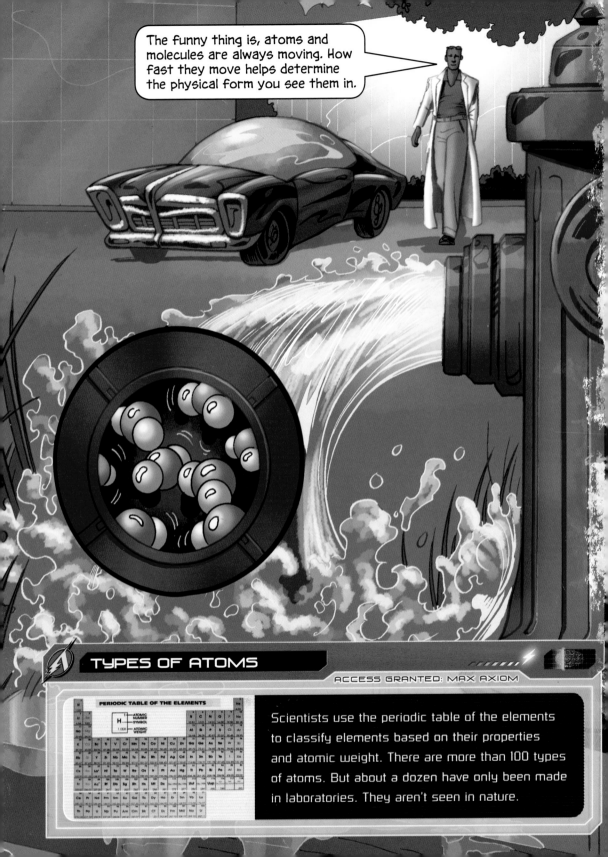

The funny thing is, atoms and molecules are always moving. How fast they move helps determine the physical form you see them in.

TYPES OF ATOMS

ACCESS GRANTED: MAX AXIOM

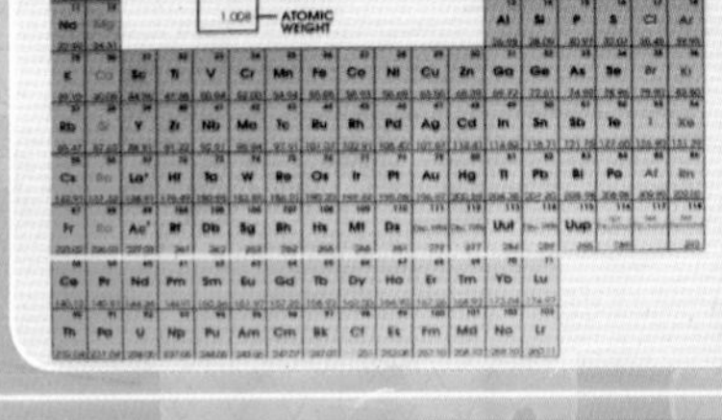

PERIODIC TABLE OF THE ELEMENTS

Scientists use the periodic table of the elements to classify elements based on their properties and atomic weight. There are more than 100 types of atoms. But about a dozen have only been made in laboratories. They aren't seen in nature.

SECTION 2 SOLIDS, LIQUIDS, AND GASES

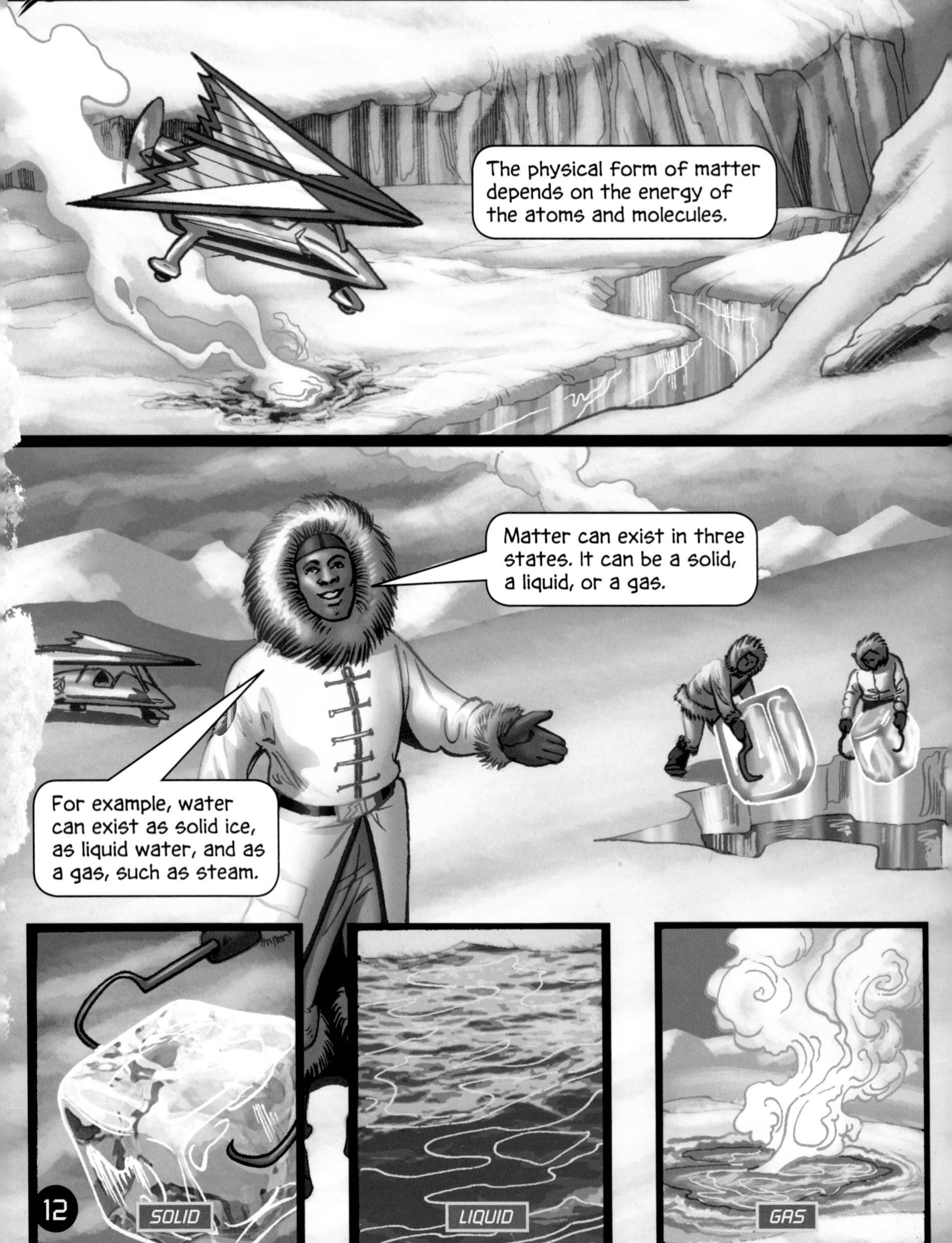

The physical form of matter depends on the energy of the atoms and molecules.
Matter can exist in three states. It can be a solid, a liquid, or a gas.
For example, water can exist as solid ice, as liquid water, and as a gas, such as steam.
SOLID
LIQUID
GAS

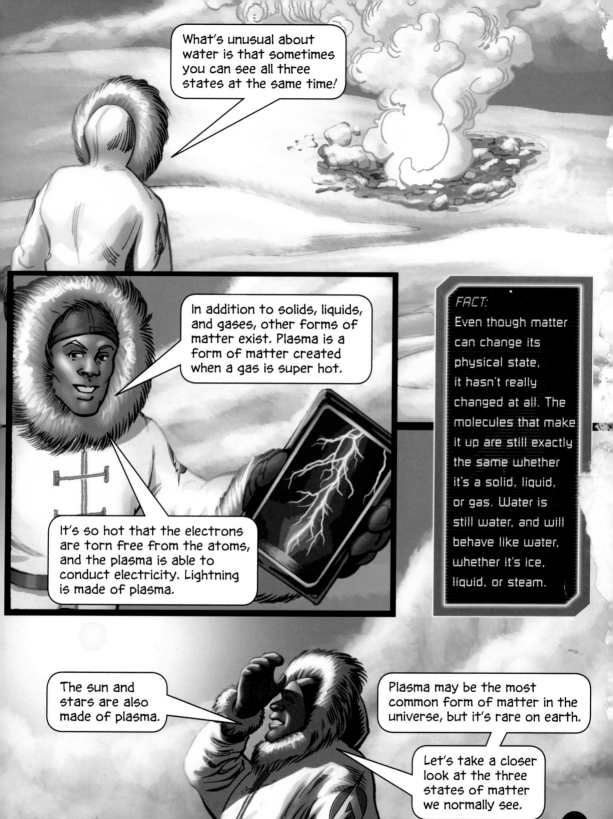

What's unusual about water is that sometimes you can see all three states at the same time!

In addition to solids, liquids, and gases, other forms of matter exist. Plasma is a form of matter created when a gas is super hot.

It's so hot that the electrons are torn free from the atoms, and the plasma is able to conduct electricity. Lightning is made of plasma.

FACT:
Even though matter can change its physical state, it hasn't really changed at all. The molecules that make it up are still exactly the same whether it's a solid, liquid, or gas. Water is still water, and will behave like water, whether it's ice, liquid, or steam.

The sun and stars are also made of plasma.

Plasma may be the most common form of matter in the universe, but it's rare on earth.

Let's take a closer look at the three states of matter we normally see.

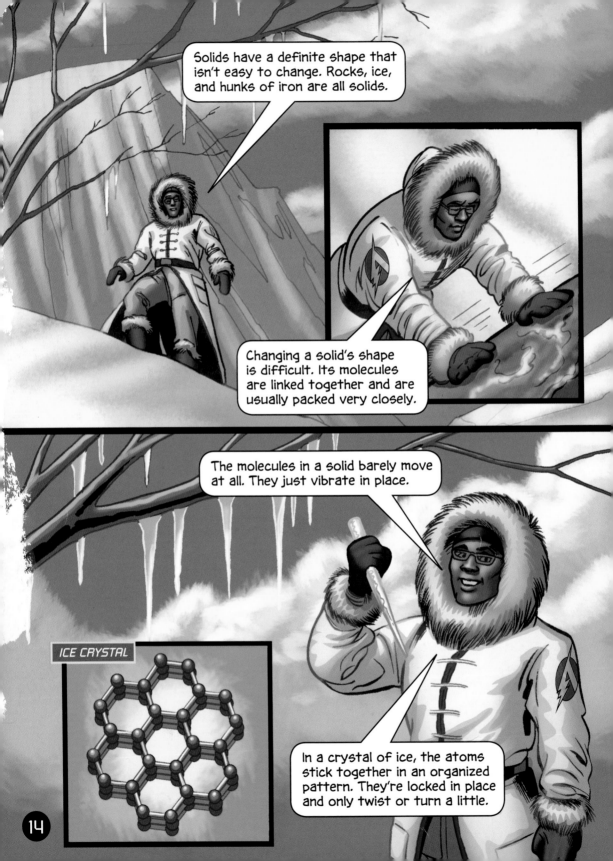

Solids have a definite shape that isn't easy to change. Rocks, ice, and hunks of iron are all solids.

Changing a solid's shape is difficult. Its molecules are linked together and are usually packed very closely.

The molecules in a solid barely move at all. They just vibrate in place.

ICE CRYSTAL

In a crystal of ice, the atoms stick together in an organized pattern. They're locked in place and only twist or turn a little.

14

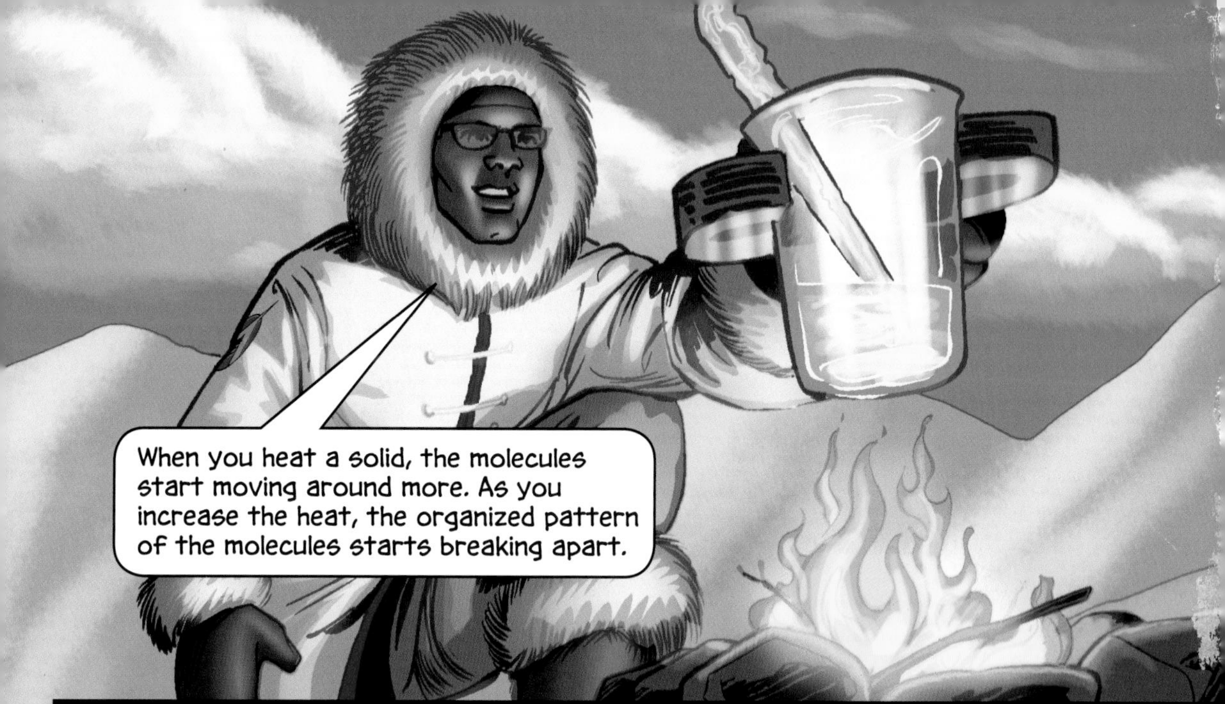
When you heat a solid, the molecules start moving around more. As you increase the heat, the organized pattern of the molecules starts breaking apart.

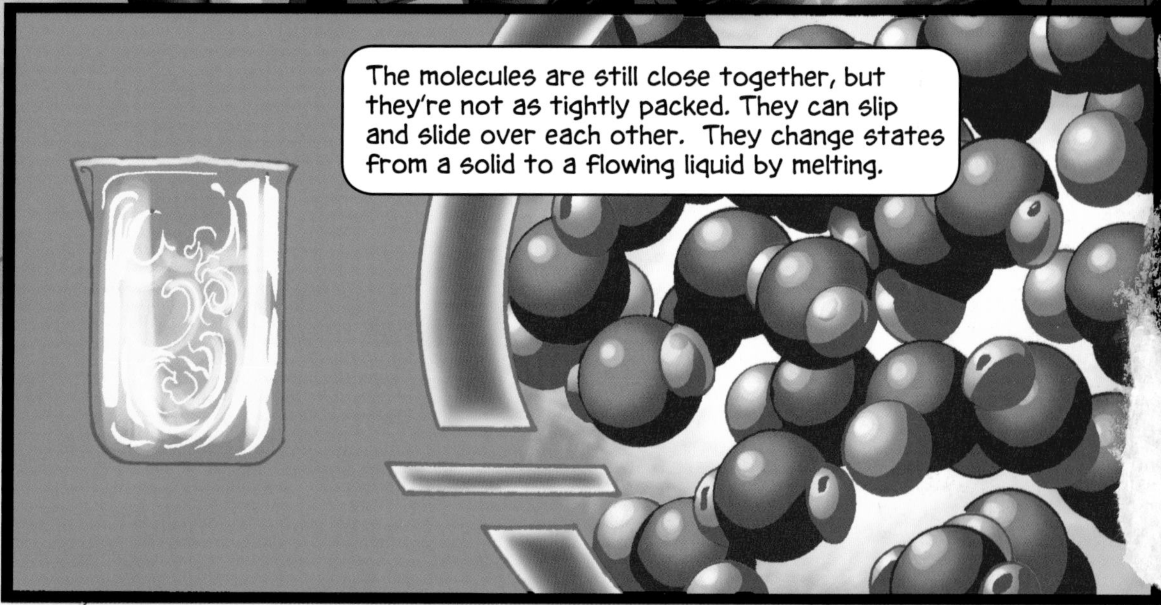
The molecules are still close together, but they're not as tightly packed. They can slip and slide over each other. They change states from a solid to a flowing liquid by melting.

MELTING ROCKS

ACCESS GRANTED: MAX AXIOM

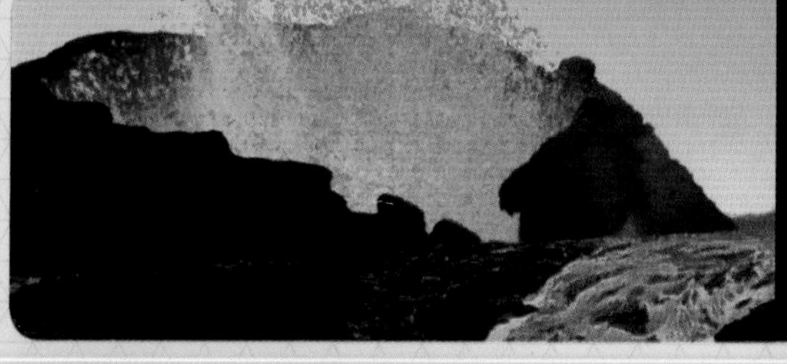

Lava, anyone? Even rocks melt at high enough temperatures. Some rocks can melt at the relatively low temperature of 1,300 to 1,500 degrees Fahrenheit, or 704 to 816 degrees Celsius.

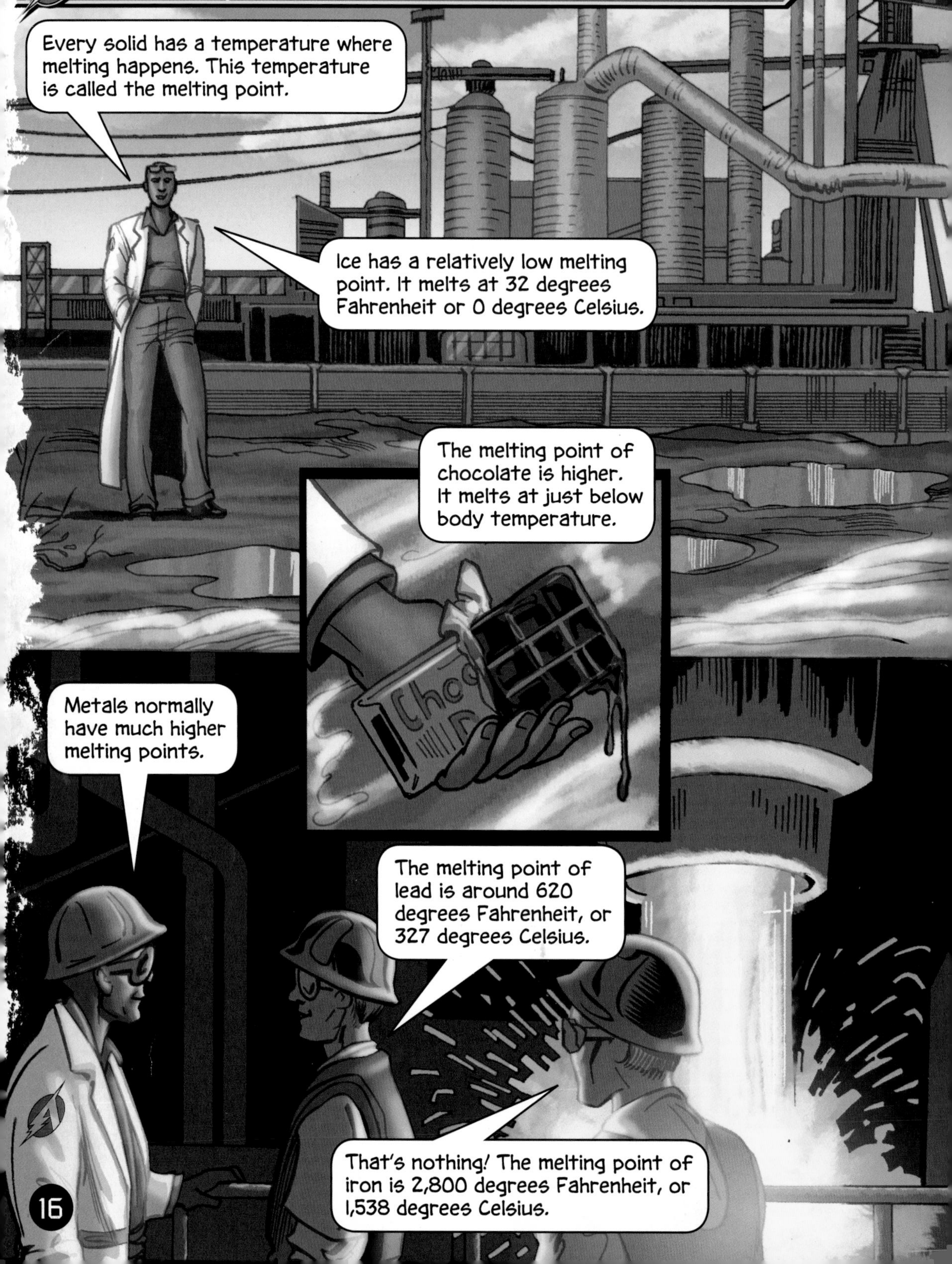
Every solid has a temperature where melting happens. This temperature is called the melting point.
Ice has a relatively low melting point. It melts at 32 degrees Fahrenheit or 0 degrees Celsius.
The melting point of chocolate is higher. It melts at just below body temperature.
Metals normally have much higher melting points.
The melting point of lead is around 620 degrees Fahrenheit, or 327 degrees Celsius.
That's nothing! The melting point of iron is 2,800 degrees Fahrenheit, or 1,538 degrees Celsius.

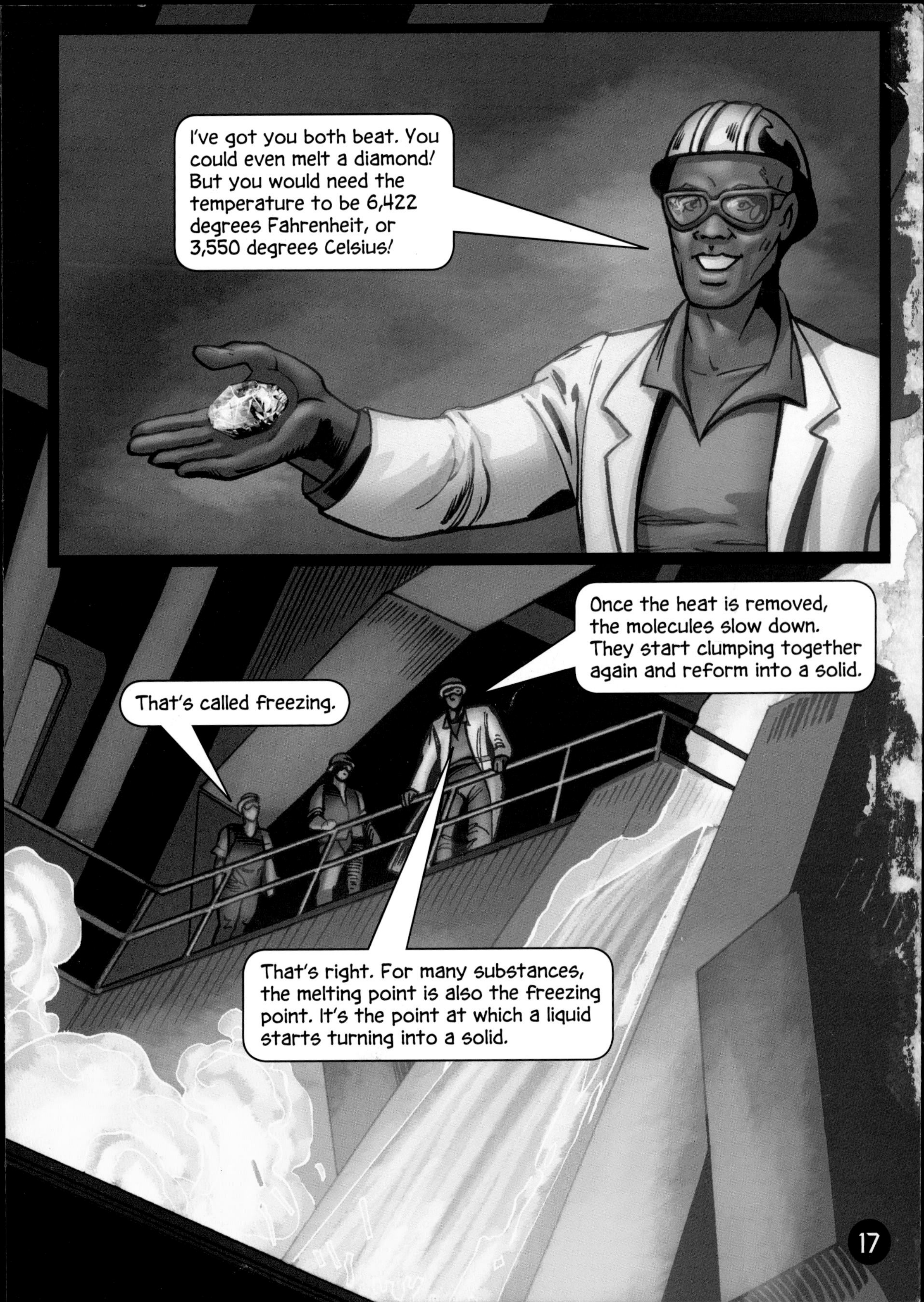
I've got you both beat. You could even melt a diamond! But you would need the temperature to be 6,422 degrees Fahrenheit, or 3,550 degrees Celsius!
Once the heat is removed, the molecules slow down. They start clumping together again and reform into a solid.
That's called freezing.
That's right. For many substances, the melting point is also the freezing point. It's the point at which a liquid starts turning into a solid.

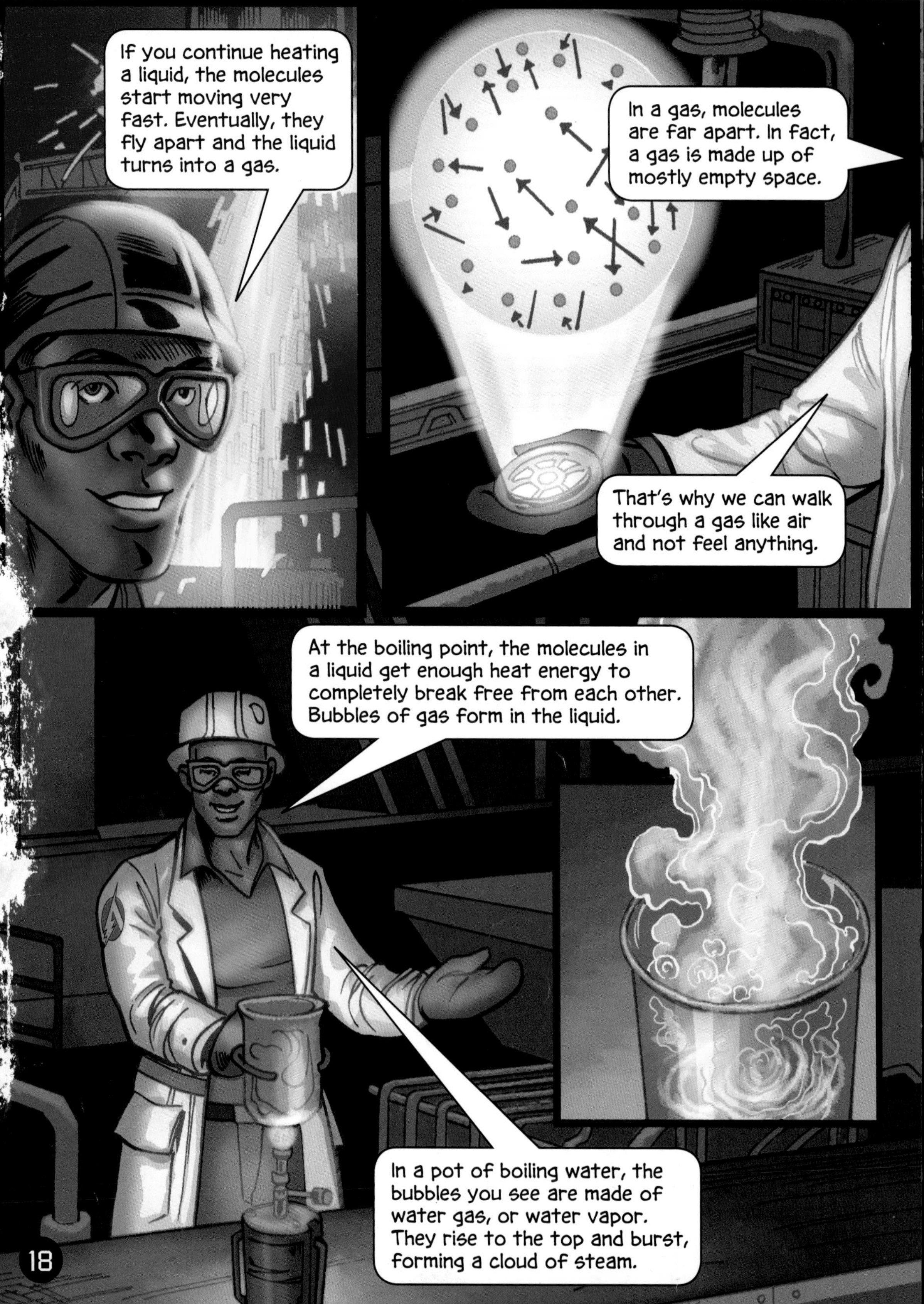
If you continue heating a liquid, the molecules start moving very fast. Eventually, they fly apart and the liquid turns into a gas.
In a gas, molecules are far apart. In fact, a gas is made up of mostly empty space.
That's why we can walk through a gas like air and not feel anything.
At the boiling point, the molecules in a liquid get enough heat energy to completely break free from each other. Bubbles of gas form in the liquid.
In a pot of boiling water, the bubbles you see are made of water gas, or water vapor. They rise to the top and burst, forming a cloud of steam.

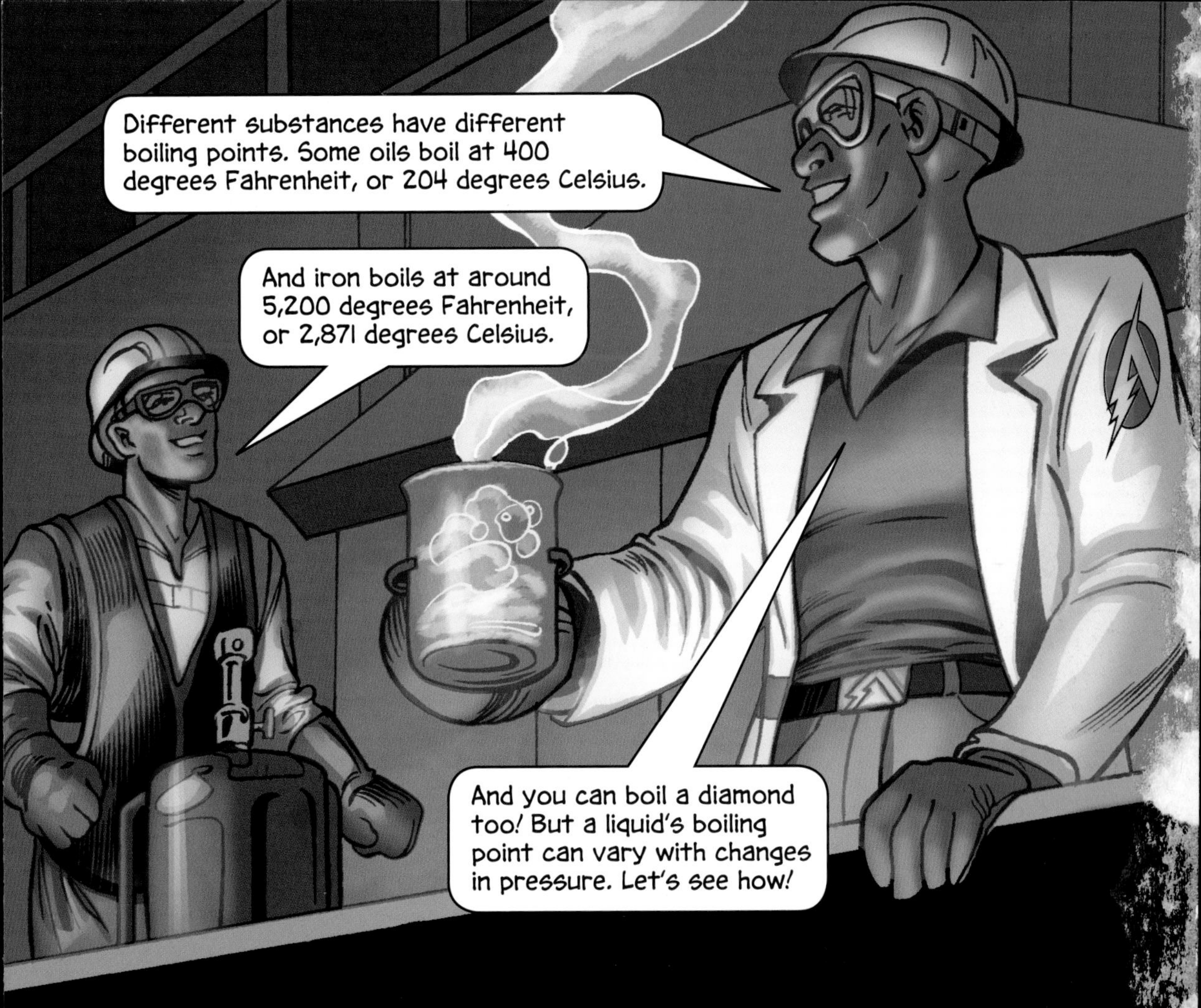
Different substances have different boiling points. Some oils boil at 400 degrees Fahrenheit, or 204 degrees Celsius.
And iron boils at around 5,200 degrees Fahrenheit, or 2,871 degrees Celsius.
And you can boil a diamond too! But a liquid's boiling point can vary with changes in pressure. Let's see how!

VOLUME

ACCESS GRANTED: MAX AXIOM

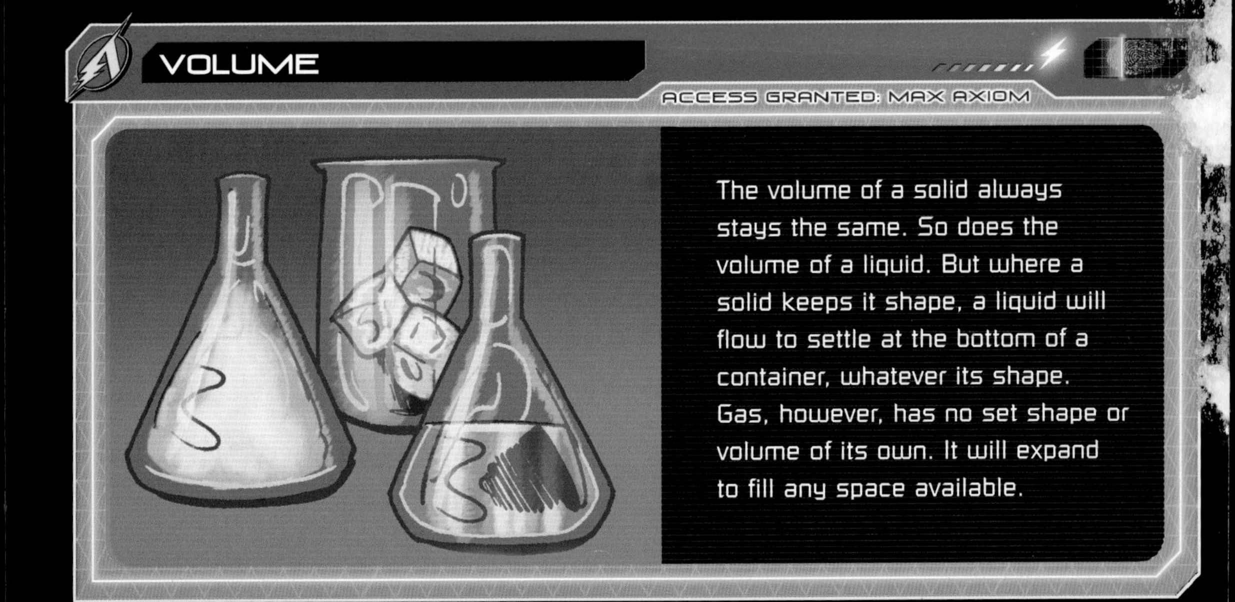

The volume of a solid always stays the same. So does the volume of a liquid. But where a solid keeps it shape, a liquid will flow to settle at the bottom of a container, whatever its shape. Gas, however, has no set shape or volume of its own. It will expand to fill any space available.

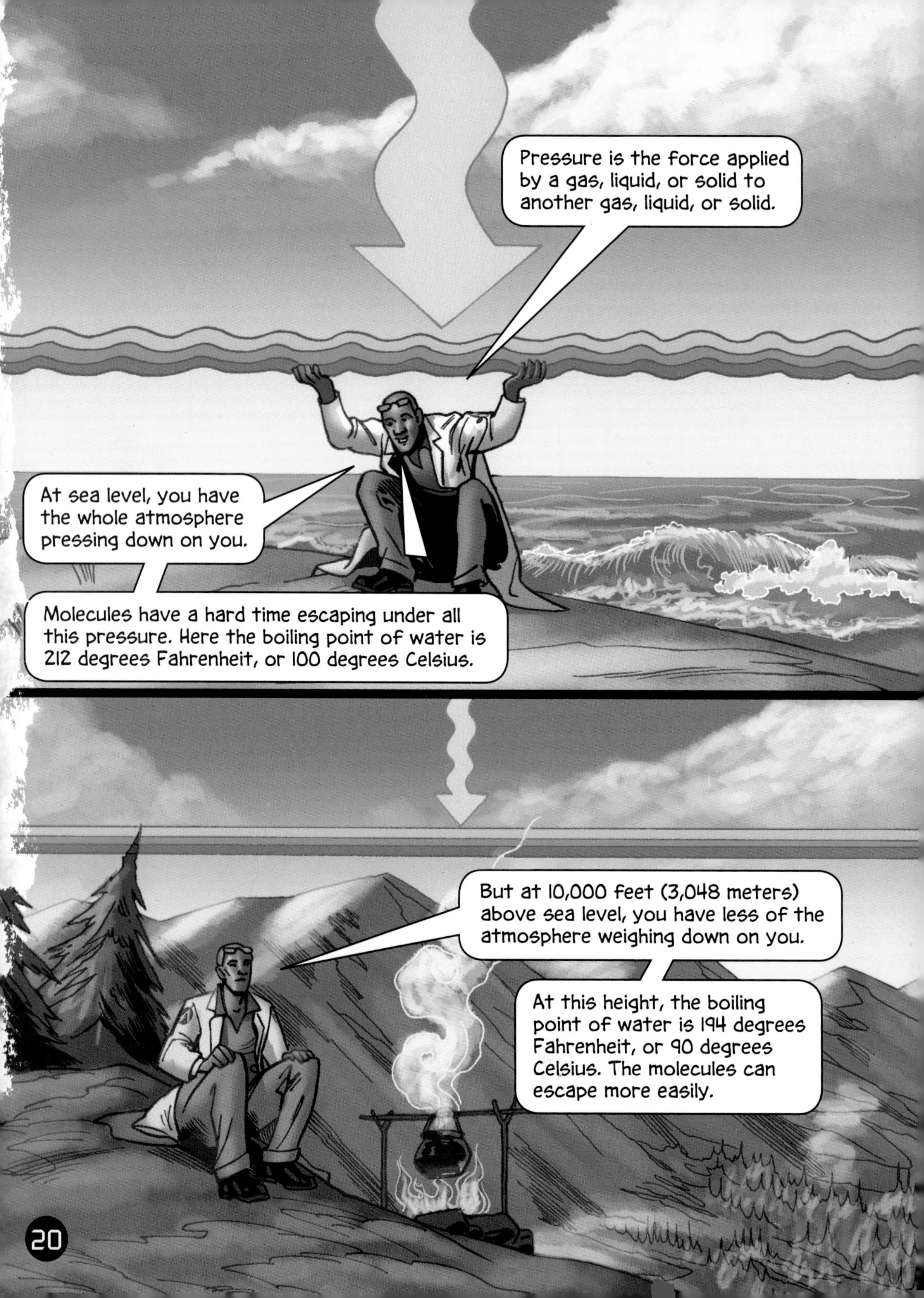
Pressure is the force applied by a gas, liquid, or solid to another gas, liquid, or solid.
At sea level, you have the whole atmosphere pressing down on you.
Molecules have a hard time escaping under all this pressure. Here the boiling point of water is 212 degrees Fahrenheit, or 100 degrees Celsius.
But at 10,000 feet (3,048 meters) above sea level, you have less of the atmosphere weighing down on you.
At this height, the boiling point of water is 194 degrees Fahrenheit, or 90 degrees Celsius. The molecules can escape more easily.

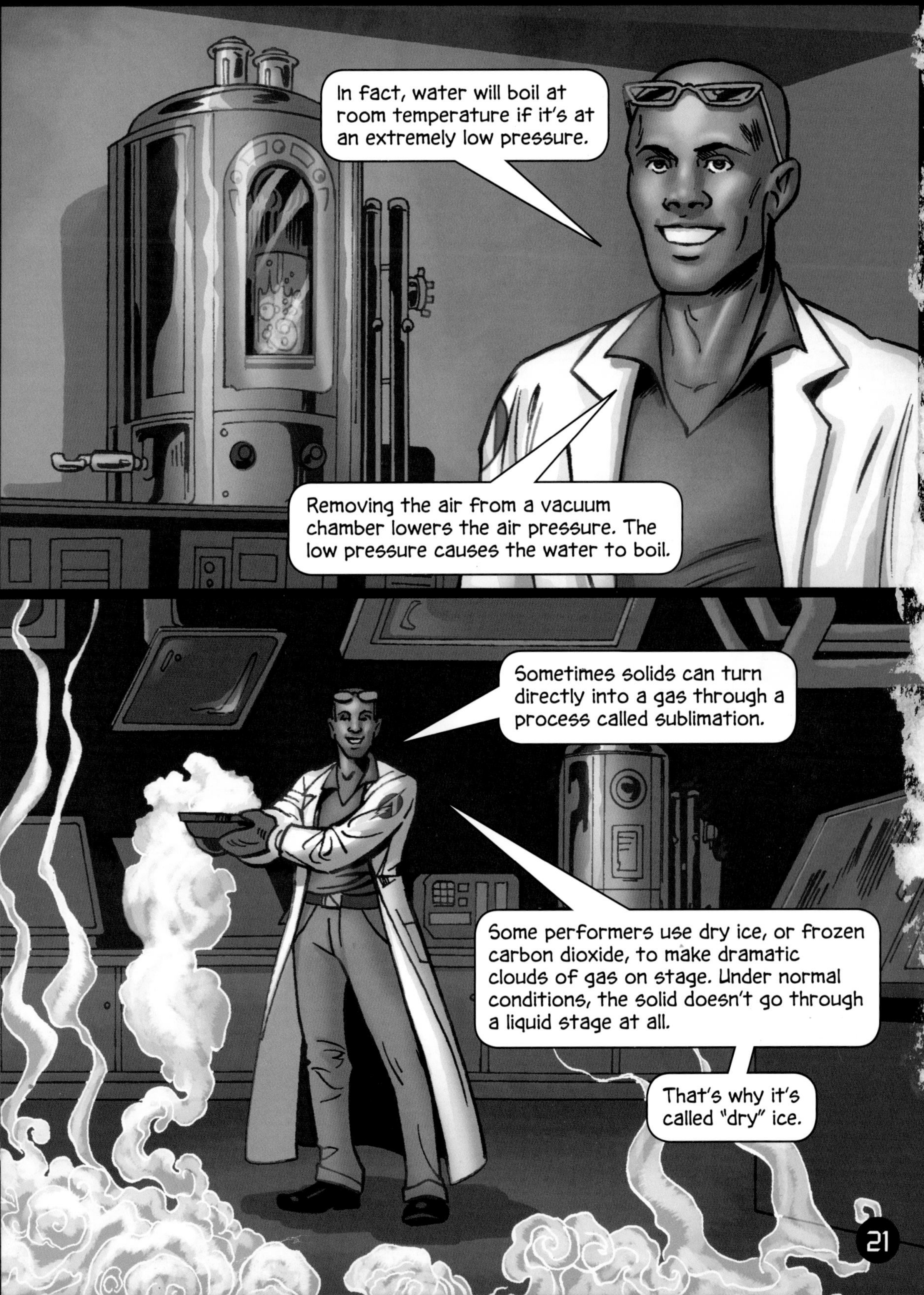
In fact, water will boil at room temperature if it's at an extremely low pressure.
Removing the air from a vacuum chamber lowers the air pressure. The low pressure causes the water to boil.
Sometimes solids can turn directly into a gas through a process called sublimation.
Some performers use dry ice, or frozen carbon dioxide, to make dramatic clouds of gas on stage. Under normal conditions, the solid doesn't go through a liquid stage at all.
That's why it's called "dry" ice.

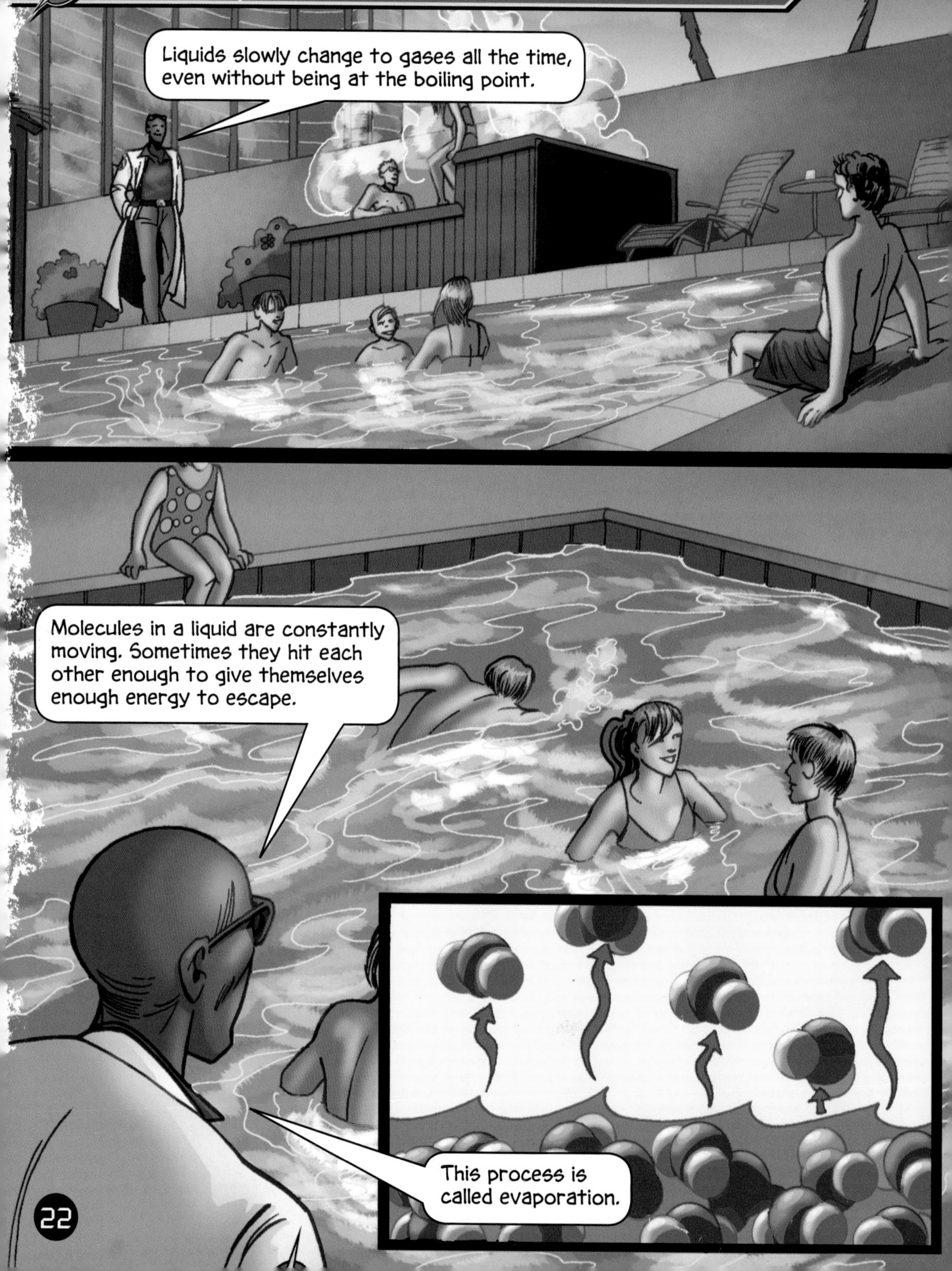
Liquids slowly change to gases all the time, even without being at the boiling point.
Molecules in a liquid are constantly moving. Sometimes they hit each other enough to give themselves enough energy to escape.
This process is called evaporation.

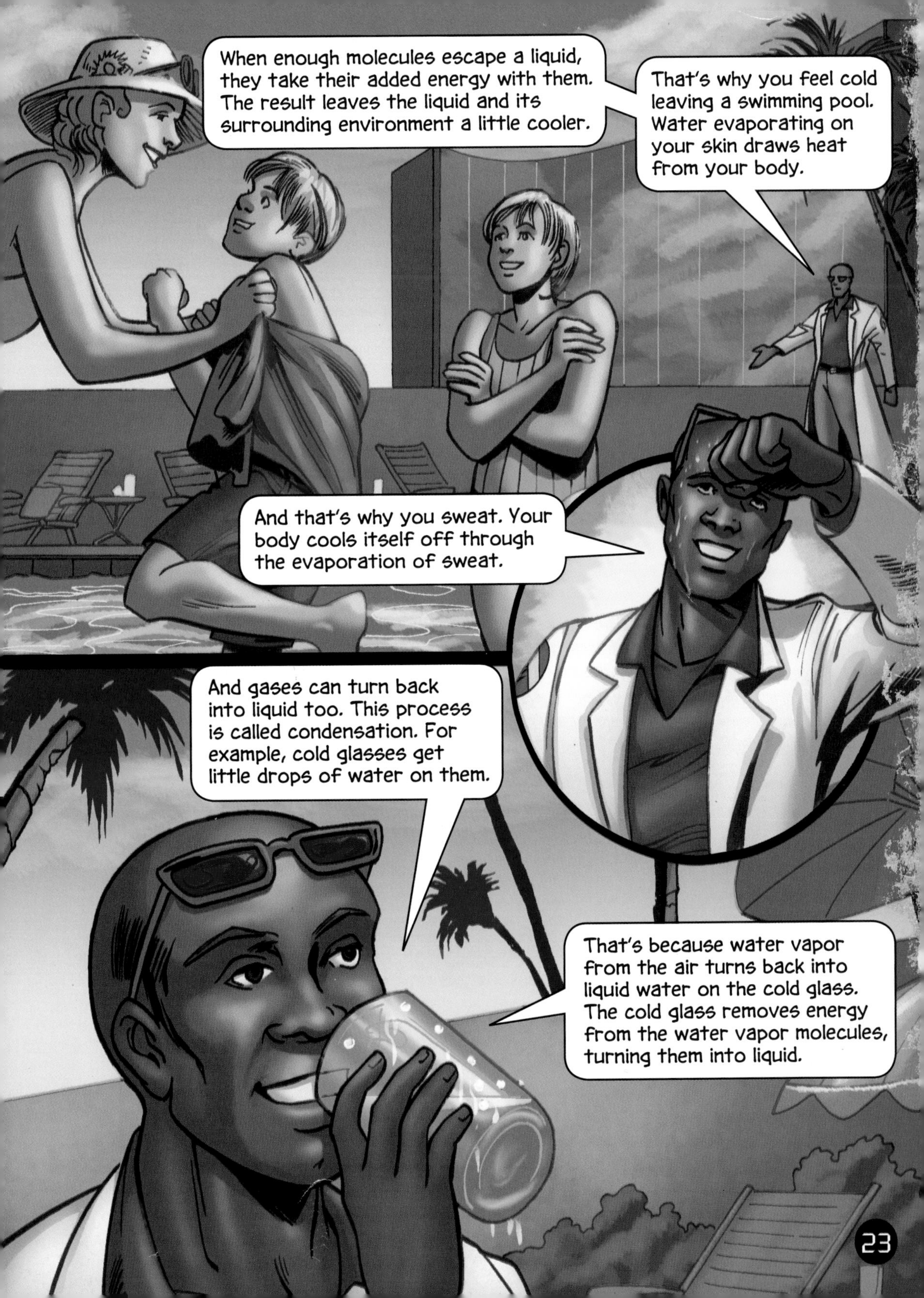
When enough molecules escape a liquid, they take their added energy with them. The result leaves the liquid and its surrounding environment a little cooler.
That's why you feel cold leaving a swimming pool. Water evaporating on your skin draws heat from your body.
And that's why you sweat. Your body cools itself off through the evaporation of sweat.
And gases can turn back into liquid too. This process is called condensation. For example, cold glasses get little drops of water on them.
That's because water vapor from the air turns back into liquid water on the cold glass. The cold glass removes energy from the water vapor molecules, turning them into liquid.

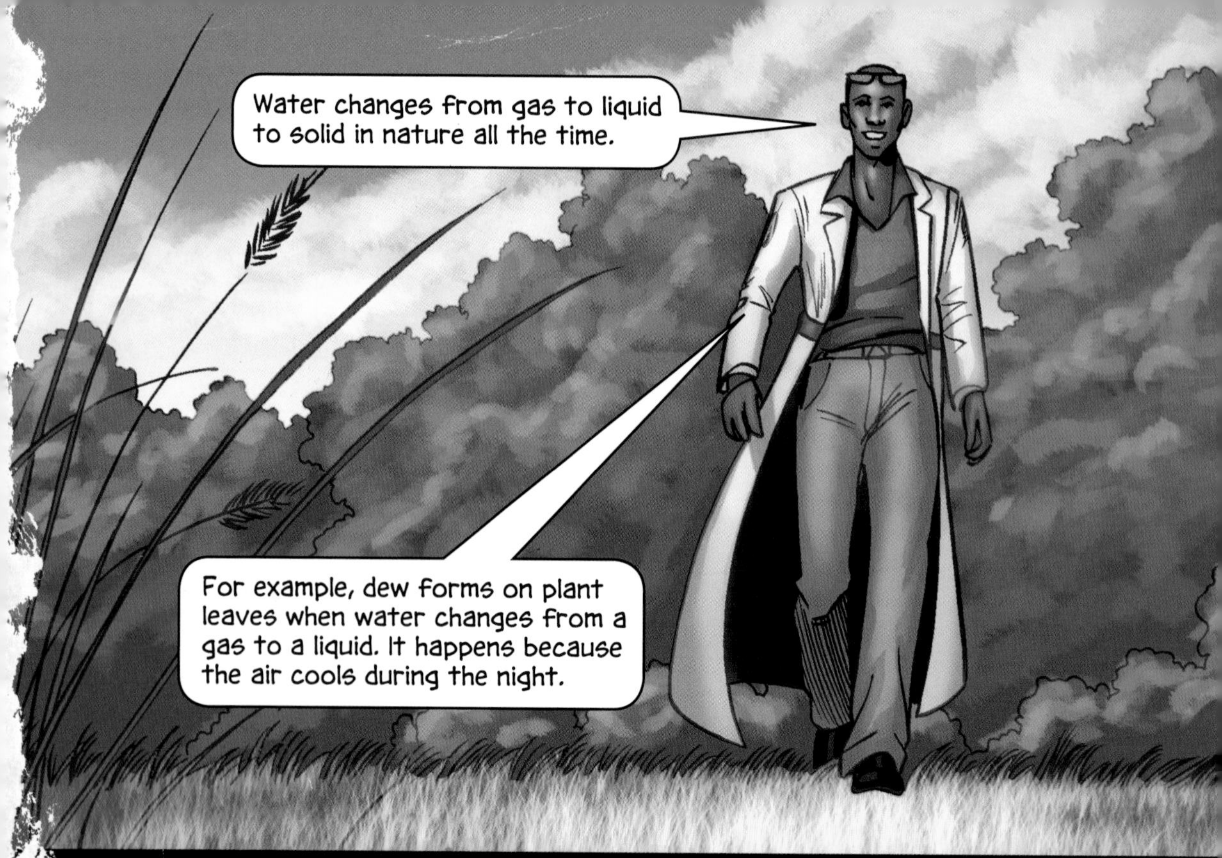
Water changes from gas to liquid to solid in nature all the time.
For example, dew forms on plant leaves when water changes from a gas to a liquid. It happens because the air cools during the night.

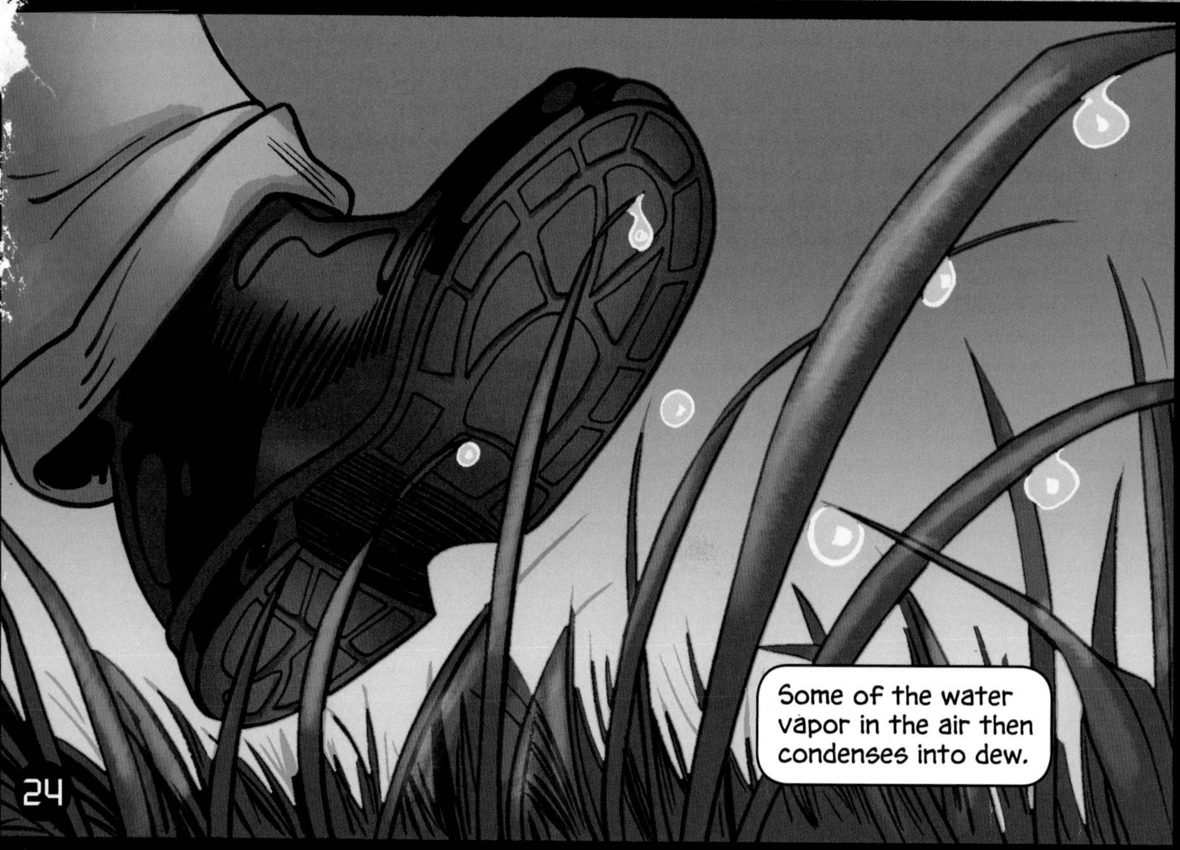
Some of the water vapor in the air then condenses into dew.

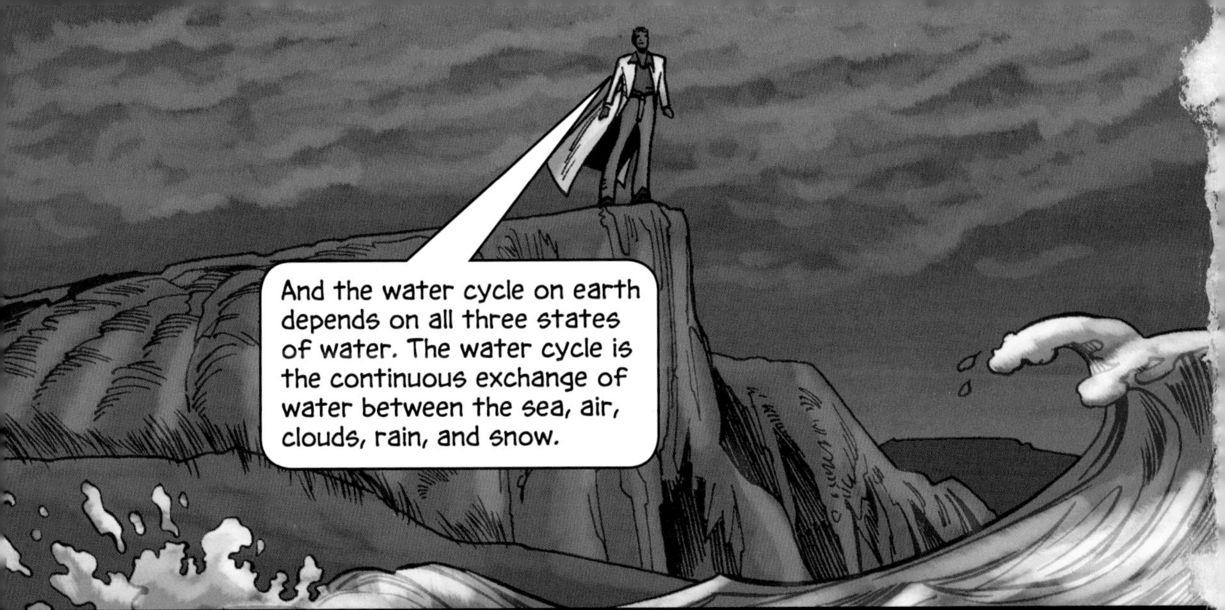

And the water cycle on earth depends on all three states of water. The water cycle is the continuous exchange of water between the sea, air, clouds, rain, and snow.

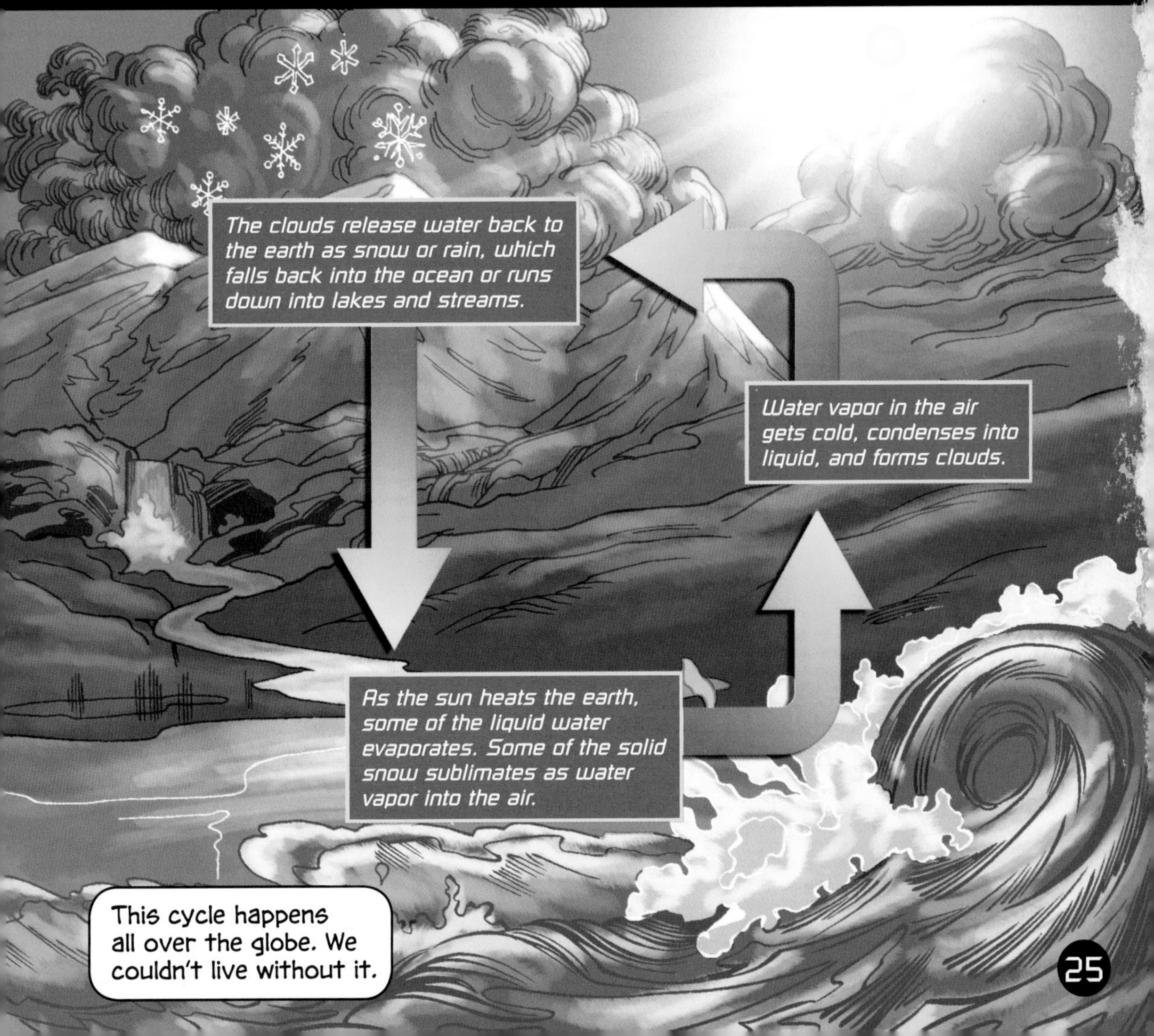

The clouds release water back to the earth as snow or rain, which falls back into the ocean or runs down into lakes and streams.
As the sun heats the earth, some of the liquid water evaporates. Some of the solid snow sublimates as water vapor into the air.
Water vapor in the air gets cold, condenses into liquid, and forms clouds.
This cycle happens all over the globe. We couldn't live without it.

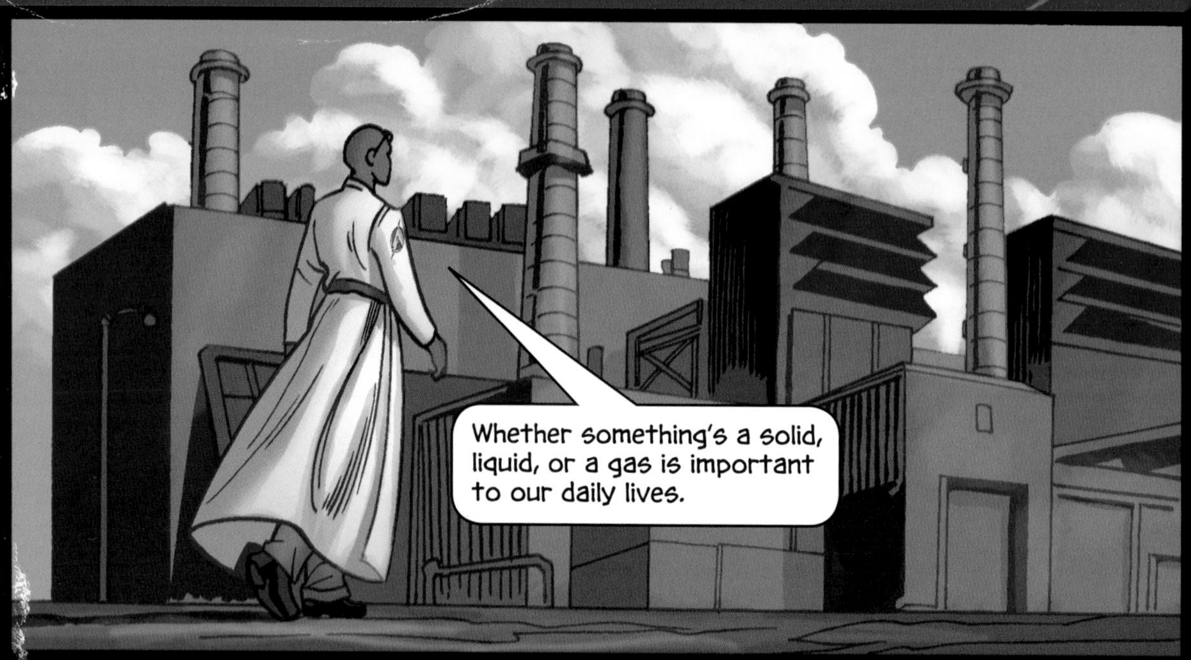
Whether something's a solid, liquid, or a gas is important to our daily lives.

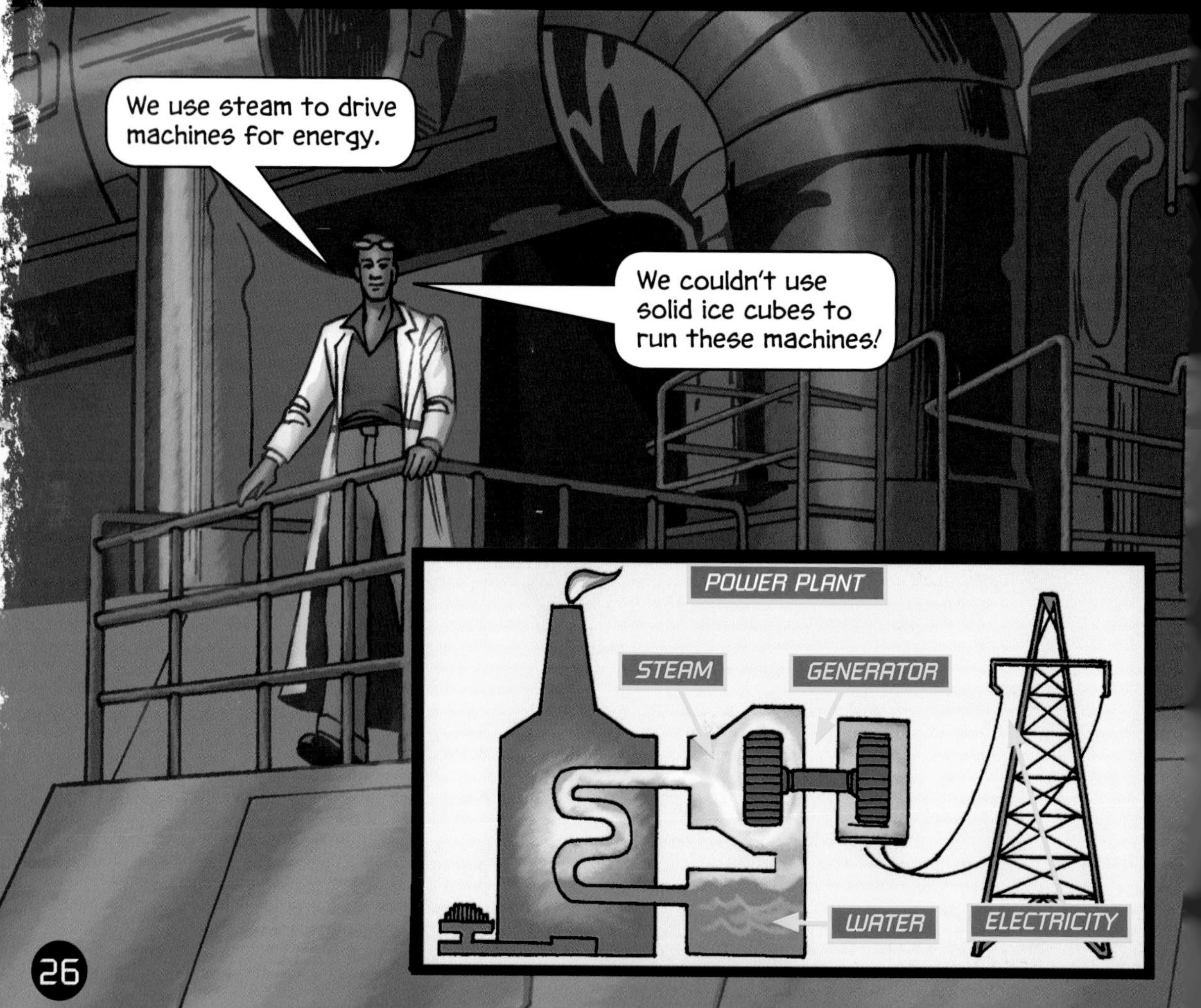
We use steam to drive machines for energy.
We couldn't use solid ice cubes to run these machines!
POWER PLANT
STEAM
GENERATOR
WATER
ELECTRICITY

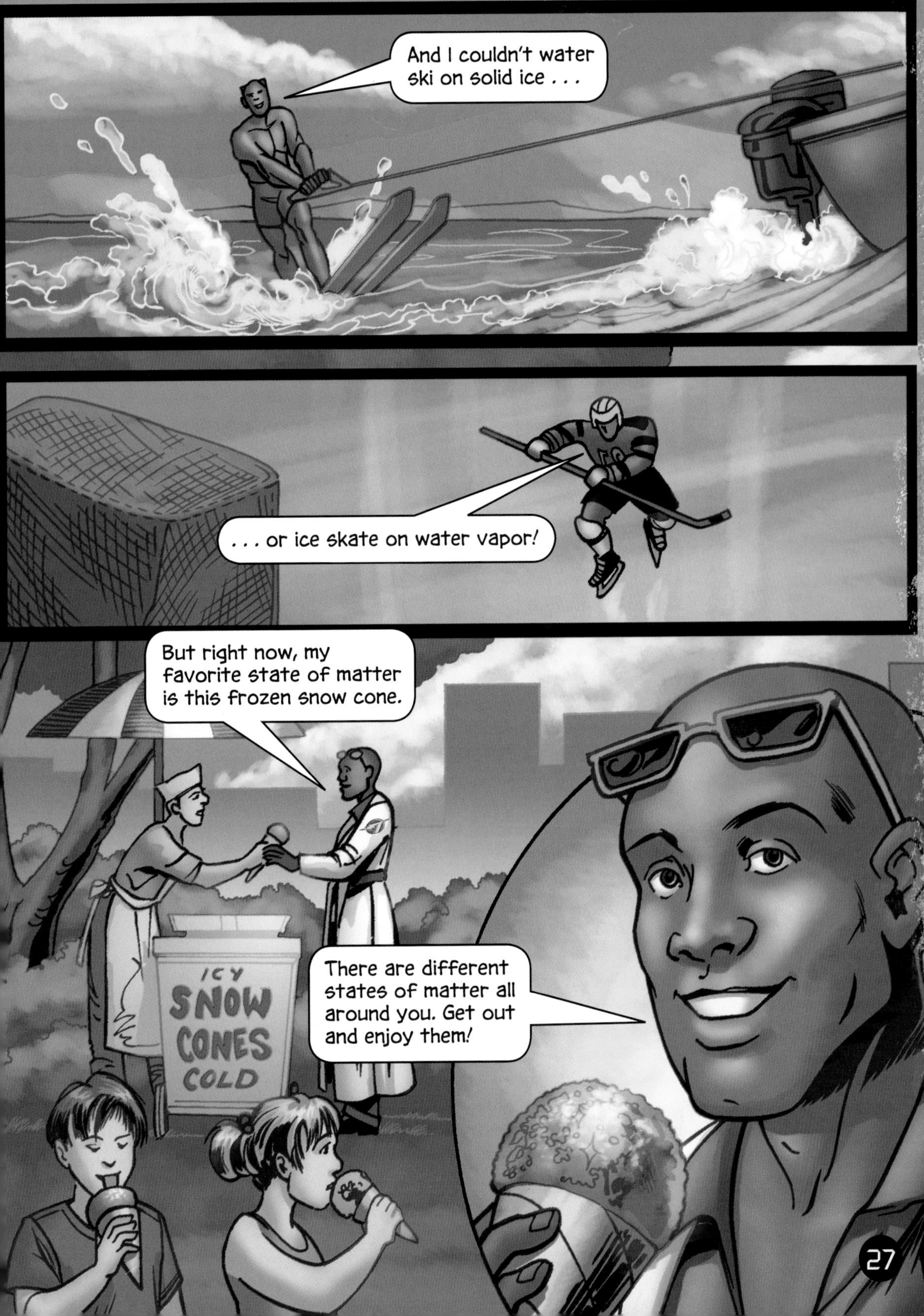
And I couldn't water ski on solid ice . . .
. . . or ice skate on water vapor!
But right now, my favorite state of matter is this frozen snow cone.
ICY SNOW CONES COLD
There are different states of matter all around you. Get out and enjoy them!

MORE ABOUT
STATES OF MATTER

More than 2,000 years ago, the Greek philosopher Leucippus came up with the idea that there was only one type of matter. He guessed that if you could cut matter up over and over again, you'd eventually get to a piece of matter you couldn't divide any further. His student Democritus called these tiny indivisible pieces of matter "atoms."

Atoms are made up of even smaller particles called protons, neutrons, and electrons. But protons and neutrons are made up of even tinier particles called quarks. Some scientists think quarks are as small as things get. Others scientsts aren't so sure. They believe quarks themselves may be made up of even smaller things called strings.

In the past few years, scientists have created two new forms of matter. These atoms are Bose-Einstein condensates and fermionic condensates. These exotic forms of matter can exist only under very special and extreme conditions in a laboratory.

It may sound like science fiction, but antimatter does exist. Scientists have created antimatter using huge, high-tech machines. Antimatter particles are like mirror images of the particles that make up our normal world. There are antimatter protons and electrons, for example, called antiprotons and positrons. A particle and its antiparticle are the same, except that they have opposite electrical charges. But if they ever meet up, watch out! The particles destroy each other and disappear in a burst of energy.

A gas can be cooled down to make it into a liquid or solid. Oxygen is normally a gas, but at minus 297 degrees Fahrenheit, or minus 183 degrees Celsius, it becomes liquid. Oxygen will become a solid at minus 362 degrees Fahrenheit, or minus 219 degrees Celsius.

 Pure substances have defined freezing points. But you can change the freezing point of a pure substance by adding an impurity, such as salt, sugar, or alcohol. For example, when salt is added to water, the freezing point of water drops by a few degrees. That's why people put salt on icy streets and roads in the winter. The salt makes it less likely the streets will ice over.

MORE ABOUT

SUPER SCIENTIST

Real name: **Maxwell J. Axiom**
Hometown: **Seattle, Washington**
Height: **6' 1"**   Weight: **192 lbs**
Eyes: **Brown**   Hair: **None**

Super capabilities: Super intelligence; able to shrink to the size of an atom; sunglasses give x-ray vision; lab coat allows for travel through time and space.

Origin: Since birth, Max Axiom seemed destined for greatness. His mother, a marine biologist, taught her son about the mysteries of the sea. His father, a nuclear physicist and volunteer park ranger, schooled Max on the wonders of earth and sky.

One day on a wilderness hike, a megacharged lightning bolt struck Max with blinding fury. When he awoke, Max discovered a newfound energy and set out to learn as much about science as possible. He traveled the globe earning degrees in every aspect of the field. Upon his return, he was ready to share his knowledge and new identity with the world. He had become Max Axiom, Super Scientist.

GLOSSARY

atmosphere (AT-muhss-fihr) — the mixture of gases that surrounds the earth

atom (AT-uhm) — an element in its smallest form

condensation (kahn-duhn-SAY-shuhn) — the act of turning from a gas into a liquid

electron (i-LEK-tron) — a tiny particle in an atom that travels around the nucleus

evaporation (i-vap-uh-RAY-shun) — the act of turning from a liquid to a gas

gravity (GRAV-uh-tee) — a force that pulls objects together; gravity pulls objects down toward the center of Earth and the Moon.

matter (MAT-ur) — anything that has weight and takes up space

molecule (MOL-uh-kyool) — the smallest part of an element that can exist and still keep the characteristics of the element

neutron (NOO-trahn) — one of the very small parts in an atom's nucleus

particle (PAR-tuh-kuhl) — a tiny piece of something

proton (PRO-tahn) — one of the very small parts in an atom's nucleus

sublimation (sub-lih-MAY-shun) — the act of turning from a solid to a gas

vapor (VAY-pur) — a gas made from something that is usually a liquid or solid at normal temperatures

volume (VOL-yuhm) — the amount of space taken up by an object

Read More

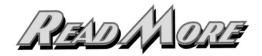

Brent, Lynnette. *States of Matter.* Why Chemistry Matters. New York: Crabtree, 2009.

Green, Dan. *Physics.* New York: Kingfisher, 2008.

Johnson, Penny. *Ice to Steam: Changing States of Matter.* Let's Explore Science. Vero Beach, Fla.: Rourke, 2008.

Spilsbury, Richard, and Louise Spilsbury. *What Are Solids, Liquids, and Gases?: Exploring Science With Hands-On Activities.* In Touch with Basic Science. Berkeley Heights, N.J.: Enslow, 2008.

Walker, Sally M. *Matter.* Early Bird Energy. Minneapolis: Lerner, 2006.

Internet Sites

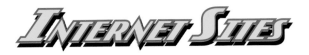

FactHound offers a safe, fun way to find educator-approved Internet sites related to this book.

Here's what you do:

1. Visit *www.facthound.com*
2. Choose your grade level.
3. Begin your search.

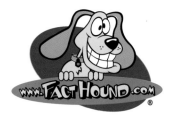

This book's ID number is 9781429623391.

FactHound will fetch the best sites for you!

air, 5, 18
antimatter, 28
atomic weight, 11
atoms, 8, 9, 10, 12, 13,
    14, 28
    types of, 11

boiling points, 18, 19, 20, 22

condensation, 23, 29

dry ice, 21

electrons, 9, 13, 28
energy, 12, 18, 22, 23, 26, 28
evaporation, 22–23

freezing points, 17, 29

gases, 12, 13, 18, 19, 20, 21, 26
    and condensation, 23, 24, 29
    and evaporation, 22

Leucippus, 28
liquids, 12, 13, 15, 19, 20,24,
    26, 29
    and boiling, 18, 19
    and evaporation, 22–23
    and freezing, 17

mass, 6–7
melting points, 16, 17

molecules
    makeup of, 8, 9, 10, 13
    movement of, 11, 12, 14, 15,
        17, 18, 20, 22, 23

neutrons, 9, 28

periodic table, 11
plasma, 13
pressure, 19, 20–21
protons, 9, 28

quarks, 28

solids, 12, 13, 14–15, 16, 17, 19,
    20, 21, 26, 29
strings, 28
sublimation, 21, 25

volume, 19

water, 12, 13, 24
    as gas, 12, 18, 23, 24, 25,
        26, 27
    as liquid, 12, 18, 20, 21, 23,
        24,25, 29
    as solid, 12, 14, 16, 24, 25,
        26, 27
    chemical makeup of, 10
water cycle, 25
weight, 7